UNDER ASSAULT:

A CRIME REPORTER'S TRUE STORY OVERCOMING SEXUAL TRAUMA & EXPOSING INJUSTICE

BY ANNA GIARITELLI

First Hardback and Paperback Edition

Some names, businesses, places, events, locales, incidents, and identifying details inside this book have been changed to protect the privacy of individuals.

Published by Freiling Agency, LLC.

P.O. Box 1264
Warrenton, VA 20188

www.FreilingAgency.com

HB ISBN: 978-1-969826-34-4
PB ISBN: 978-1-969826-33-7
E-book ISBN: 978-1-969826-35-1

DEDICATION

This book is dedicated to every girl and woman who has been sexually harassed or assaulted. Whether you reported it or not, it happened, and it changed you. This is my story, but it's also *our* story as women.

CONTENTS

Introduction vii

Chapter 1 The Girl Next Door 1

Chapter 2 The Washington Days 11

Chapter 3 The Attack 21

Chapter 4 The Aftermath 37

Chapter 5 The Initial Recovery 51

Chapter 6 The Cover-up 67

Chapter 7 The Return to Washington 79

Chapter 8 The Final Straw 93

Chapter 9 The Texan Transplant 103

Chapter 10 The Grand Jury 115

Chapter 11 The Border Crisis 125

Chapter 12 The East Coast Return 135

Chapter 13 Living a Comeback Story 157

Acknowledgments 179

INTRODUCTION

"All along you were blooming."
Morgan Harper Nichols

April 4th used to be a day that I dreaded months before its arrival every year.

On April 4, 2020, I was physically and sexually assaulted in public not far from the U.S. Capitol in Washington, D.C.

That terrible day has been redeemed in a way that I never imagined was possible.

I did not believe back then that the hell-on-earth experience and the years of recovery that followed could turn into something that I would look back on with gratitude to have suffered through.

But it did when I faced what I had lost, the humiliation I endured, and the shame of what a man did to me. All of the suffering has been and continues to be redeemed.

Your worst moment in life could actually become the one that you are the most thankful for, which changes your life infinitely for the better. It certainly was for me.

When I was in the ninth grade, the girls in my public school gym class were pulled from our normal second-period physical education to an overflow classroom for a lecture.

The presenter stated to a roomful of about two dozen girls: "One-in-three of you will be sexually assaulted in your lifetime."

I remember telling myself that I would not be the one-in-three. Rape and assault were life-ruiners. I didn't know anything about trauma or what it was like to be the victim of such a crime, but it seemed that it would be like the end of the world. There was no way that I could end up a victim. I had dreams and plans—nothing would get in my way.

Twenty-two years later, I am not sure what the purpose of that class presentation was or who came up with it. The adults in the class had showed us self-defense moves. I don't remember any of the moves, but that "one-in-three" line has lived in my head for more than two decades.

I couldn't have imagined that I would be the one-in-three. Now, as a thirty-six-year-old woman, I'm convinced that the one-in-three statistic is actually far higher.

While this book is about what I went through as a sexual assault victim in Washington, D.C., that assault in 2020 was not the first time I was a victim of sexual violence.

On three occasions in my thirty-six years, I have been manipulated, assaulted, or attacked in a sexual manner. If another woman had told me that about herself, I may have viewed her as having *asked for it*. I had been convinced by society that violence against a woman is the woman's fault. Women are hard on one another—sometimes we do not cut any slack for our own kind after one is tricked into sex or if she is assaulted by a stranger. Maybe it is because we do not want to admit how bad things really are—that no matter what we do to protect ourselves, it is not always possible. We would rather blame other women for being too loose or for setting themselves up for it than admit things are actually as bad as they are. Is that not the more terrifying reality?

Despite all of this, I have chosen to share my journey as a woman who was sexually harassed, propositioned, and assaulted because I know that my experiences are not rare.

It's a club that no one wants to be a member of—the "Yeah, a guy did something like that to me, but I'm just trying to move on now" club.

You may have picked up this book out of curiosity, because you recognized one of the people who endorsed it on the cover, or because you read a viral op-ed about how D.C. police covered up my crime.

You may be reading this book because someone did something morally and criminally wrong to you or to someone you love—something that was not deserved. I'll say it again: *something that you did not deserve or ask for.*

Sexual trauma can have a mystifying hold on a victim that is hard to put into words in conversations with others, much less in her own head. She knows that she would never be the same after that day. She changed, but she does not know how. She does not know why something that happened years ago can still bother her so much.

I know that feeling.

After being attacked on the street in 2020, I could tell you in great detail about the facts of the actual event, but I was at a loss for words in therapy when I attempted to describe how it had changed *me.*

I couldn't put a finger on how I changed, but the emotional impact was clear. Back when I first considered writing a book in 2022, I was still angry. Angry was an understatement. I was angry and humiliated for having been a victim in a very public sexual assault on the street by a man. I was furious with the police in Washington, D.C., after learning that the crime stats posted on their website omitted my assault and painted a safer picture of the city than was reality. I was still confused about why the man who hurt me that day had targeted me. I was so angry that for several years, whenever someone mentioned Washington, I would tell them, "We should burn that place down."

Cringe.

I walked around for years with so much hatred in my heart for the men who have hurt me, especially after 2020. It was not just about a man who assaulted me; it was also about my hometown turning its back on me. It felt as though Washington—the place that meant more to me than my industry or friends in that city—turned its back on me.

The life that I had been building for seven years in Washington was taken from me in an instant. My career hinged on my ability to live in that city. After choosing to leave in 2021, I became a nomad overnight, working remotely for a Washington company, unsure how I could continue in my career while living outside of the nation's capital. It worked during the pandemic only because everyone else was working from home, but what would happen to me when we all had to return to the office?

I was angry that my assault would have a lifelong impact on me. The man who attacked me got a short prison sentence, but as the victim, I had been sentenced to my life being forever changed. Where's the justice in that? He had gotten off a lot easier than I had, and he was the guilty one.

And I was angry with God. As someone who believed in Him before the 2020 attack, I wondered incessantly for the first few years why He let this happen to me and how He could possibly use it for good in my life, as the Bible promises that He will.

Four years after the attack in Washington, on April 4, 2024, I took to Twitter (now X) and disclosed that I had been sexually assaulted in downtown Washington. I added that I would begin writing a book about that experience and how it had changed me.

I had thought for several years about writing about my recovery journey, but I did not want to face it again. Therapy was exhausting—why make myself face all of the trauma again? It seemed like torture, not the clarifying process those around me suggested it could be.

But as I tweeted that day in 2024, seated on the top floor of WeWork's office space on Barton Springs Road in Austin, Texas, overlooking the city's skyline, I had no fear, but only courage. I decided then and there that I would write my story, even if only for my own fulfillment and for my own eyes to see.

Getting a book published seemed impossible, and it terrified me. Getting an op-ed published by a news outlet in Washington, even by my employer, scared me. I could write news stories, but I didn't know the first thing about writing an opinion piece or a book. I believed that I was the only one who cared about what I had been through. My attack and the fallout from it seemed to be my personal problems. I feared that sharing them would come off as trite and attention-seeking.

"One-in-three."

The memory of that sentence haunted me on April 4, 2024, as I tweeted. It haunted me as much as it had years earlier when it was first spoken at gym class in Wantagh High School.

Fast forward from high school to this decade. In 2021, the World Health Organization found that one-in-three women globally has been subjected to physical or sexual violence.

As of 2025, the National Sexual Violence Resource Center reported that one-in-five women in the United States has experienced completed or attempted rape during her lifetime.

So I took a leap, not knowing *if* I would land. I tweeted that I was writing a book. I knew that I would never write it if I did not publicly hold myself accountable. I could not have imagined the two years that would follow that declaration.

I spent many hours in therapy in the first three years after the attack in 2020. Each woman helped me at different points in my recovery to get to the place where I am today. I am now ready and willing to talk, having forgiven myself and those who hurt me.

The support of a few people was critical in getting me to where I am today, but the one who deserves the most thanks is myself. I say that humbly yet confidently. Here's why.

Only one person has a say in where you go and how you respond after a personal tragedy. That can be an unfortunate truth if you are not willing to accept it, but once you accept that you are the only one who can save yourself, it's no longer unfortunate. It's empowering. It is a moment that you will recognize as the beginning of your comeback story.

In recovering from any sort of trauma, recovery is not a split-second decision. It is a constant reframing of the mind. I had to choose day in and day out to keep going. In those thousands of little moments, I did not feel that I was making progress, but eventually I saw it. Almost all at once I realized how far I had come.

For me, it has been many moments of saying, "I will fight for myself. I don't even know how to fight or what that looks like, but I will keep moving forward."

Around the time of my 2020 attack, I had become familiar with artist and poet Morgan Harper Nichols. One of her best-known poetry lines is this: "All along you were blooming."

I became familiar with her work when I read those five words, the first of hers I ever read, and my knee-jerk reaction to that phrase was not positive.

Blooming? A more accurate description would be "All along, I've been suffering," from being assaulted in high school in 2007 to being seriously harassed by a boss in Washington to being attacked on the street in 2020. When would I bloom? Why were others blooming and not me?

It was not until I was willing to accept my whole story, as opposed to pushing it under the rug or minimizing it, that I was able to say, "Some of the things I have faced in my life are still indescribably awful, and I hate that they happened to me, but I accept that they are in my past and that I am responsible for how I respond to them," that the healing—and the blooming—began.

As I look back on the past six years, I imagine a field of my favorite flowers in bloom—tulips, peonies, roses. The blooms symbolize the thousands of decisions that I made to move forward.

Now, imagine your favorite flower or tree, first just one, and then a field full of them. Each one of those flowers, trees, or plants is a moment in your future in which your decision to believe in yourself and accept the past is serving your best interest. Each moment you choose to move toward healing and seeing the horrible thing that happened to you as truly in the past and not indicative of your future, a new bud pops in or a new branch leaps out from a tree.

And the best part? Every bloom represents a moment that you chose to move toward acceptance. And in doing so, you were empowered to help others do the same.

As you begin, you mostly likely won't feel that you are healing or accepting the past, or that it makes a difference.

But you are making progress, hour by hour, day by day. You'll know this when you see someone who reminds you of the person who hurt you and you begin to feel a panic attack coming on, but you decide to take deep breaths and distract yourself rather than letting yourself sink into an hours-long ordeal that leaves you succumbing to anxiety and fear.

You're growing when you decide you will get up off the couch and go for a short walk outside when the sun starts to go down because you deserve to walk the streets, day and night, not fearing the dark.

You're growing when you log into your health insurance company's website and look at therapists covered under your insurance and screenshot a few who you think might be a good fit.

You're growing when Valentine's Day is coming, and instead of wallowing in your sad story or singleness, you decide that you want to help other single women in your city feel loved and remembered, so you plan a fun night to have girlfriends over and celebrate their friendships.

All of these are real-life examples that came to mind from my own experience when I chose to accept where I was and did not wallow in the "woe is me" attitude that can easily become a habit after surviving trauma.

It's really easy to stay in victim mode. And it's a lot easier to stay there when you already know how to function in it.

It's not a "fake it until you make it" mentality as much as it is refusing to endlessly live in what had hurt me. In doing so, I became empowered and self-aware to continue making these changes. I still don't know what the end result is; I just know I'm nobody's victim anymore. I'm also no longer my own victim of self-sabotage and helplessness.

When I first shared a few sentences about my crime story in 2024, I felt inadequate as a victim. It's easy to feel inadequate. Someone who has been through a "worse" crime should speak, not me. Someone who is a regular person, not a homeland security reporter, should speak out about it. Someone who has a better story than me … you get the picture.

But God allowed me to go through this. He also saved me, not just on that day but also in the days after the attack when sometimes, frankly, I struggled to keep living.

God saved me, and I choose to talk about it now.

So here I am, a violent crime survivor, ready to talk about how God sustained me as I walked through my own valley of death, believing that God will use my story to help others to not just survive but thrive.

But accepting and forgiving are hard. They take time. Truly, time is part of healing.

How many millions of women in America have been victims of sexual assault to varying degrees and in various situations, but cannot admit to themselves that it changed them. Short of that admission, they cannot recover, so they are stuck, unsure how to move on.

How many women disappear in the middle of life and no one knows why? They seem to suddenly drop out of life, or quit the dream job, or leave the big city, or get a divorce.

What you have gone through and are going through may feel that it is not a big deal. But millions of women in this country right now feel the same way as you—the way I used to feel.

I hope by reading my story, you will find reassurance that you are not the only woman who has been hurt or felt lost in her own mind while dealing with sexual assault or felt misunderstood by your friends and family in that process. I hope this book puts words to something that you had not been able to explain until now.

It is no coincidence this book was released on April 4, 2026—six years to the day since what was once the worst day of my life. It has been a winding journey, but it has proven that I am more than someone who survived sexual assault. I am someone who went on to thrive and to make a bad day into a grand one.

I hope that you will have your own April 4, 2026, one day.

Prove me right.

CHAPTER 1

THE GIRL NEXT DOOR

My story began in Colorado. I was born in Denver and grew up in the county outside Queens borough on Long Island. My home was a wonderful place filled with love and support. I never missed a meal, got tucked in bed every night, played outside with neighbor kids, and always had a parent at home with me.

I grew up as the daughter of a minister, though I prefer the term "pastor." My father is a provider and man of wisdom who I still look up to. My mother is full of love, acceptance, and forgiveness. I consider my foundational years to have been a gift compared to what some children experience at home.

In elementary school, I read. I was a voracious reader and writer, far more than the average kid.

Those who knew me back then would not be surprised that I now write for a living, given my love for it over the past three decades.

In ninth grade, I transferred schools, from South Shore Christian School to Wantagh High School. I joined the student newspaper and became an associate editor in tenth grade. I loved to write and contribute to the publication. I felt that I was part of something that mattered. I worked with a team of students who were as passionate as I was about sharing news in written form.

At the end of tenth grade, my family moved across the country to a suburb of Portland, Oregon, for my father's job. I was not one to act out or make problems, but in the second half of my senior year of high school, I started acting out. I was curious about the world around me and frustrated by the boundaries my parents had set so I chose to try the things that some of my peers seemed to have fun doing: staying out all night, drinking, smoking, hooking up. I walked into that environment as innocent as could be and was there initially as an onlooker, but quickly became a participant. I had no idea what I was in for.

My closest high school friend had a car. We each told our parents we were sleeping over at the other's house. In reality, we would go out to parties that we had heard about at school, where we met people who would invite us to more parties outside our town and with people we did not know, often adults. If we did not sleep on a couch where we had partied, we would find a parking lot and sleep in my friend's car after the party. Every week, we drove a little further, tried a new alcohol, talked to new people. It was exciting and I could not get enough of this new world.

It was in this phase as a seventeen-year-old girl that I was assaulted by a twenty-one-year-old man. I had been intoxicated, high for the first time, and at an apartment the next town over from mine when this man made a move. He took me out to his parked Jeep in the middle of the night, away from everyone else inside. I had no understanding of what was to come as I had never had a boyfriend or been sexually active. He opened the back and told me to get in and hopped in behind me and pulled the back door shut.

I shook uncontrollably throughout the encounter. He repeatedly told me to stop shaking.

I physically felt paralyzed. I could not get up from being on my back even though I did not want to be there, but I also did not know where to go. I could not call my high school friend to come get me—she was home and could not sneak back out. I felt that I could not call my parents in that moment and explain why I was in this situation. They had believed that I was at a high school friend's sleepover. Despite being in a horrible situation, I feared my parents more at the time than I feared the effect of what I went through in that Jeep.

When that encounter finally ended a couple of hours later, I was relieved. It was over. We crawled out from the back of the Jeep and walked back to the mutual friend's apartment. I was still disoriented from the alcohol and marijuana. He showed me where I could sleep on the couch in the living room that night. He said good night and went to sleep in a spare bedroom.

He seemed to be embarrassed or ashamed of me—good enough to bring me out to his car in the night, but not even worthy of sleeping in a bed. I felt disregarded and thrown away. My head was spinning as I tried to make sense of what had just happened. I could still feel in my body what he had done to me, but mentally I was in a state of shock that it had happened.

What happened in his Jeep was nothing I had fathomed as being possible prior to that night. I had never watched porn and only knew what I had heard about from high school friends. I felt so ashamed in my body that night. I wanted to hide. As much as I wanted to go home in that moment, I was also scared to see my parents. I felt that if my parents saw me, they would know something about me was different.

I felt dirty. I believed I was dirty. I wanted to shower, but I knew that no shower could clean off this feeling.

I felt as though I had asked for it. I had smoked pot for the first time and drank. I was not in a physical state to know what I was doing when I had agreed to go with him to his car.

When college had come around, I applied and was accepted to what was then called Asbury College in Wilmore, Kentucky. (It is now Asbury University.) Asbury was a leading media communications school, which meant that it had a great undergraduate program for students interested in the media, movies and films, music, and writing. I did not know what I was going to study in college when I began my freshman year in the fall of 2007, but I knew that writing would be a big part of what I did with my life.

College was a self-discovery period, as it is for many young adults. I took a full semester of classes and worked up to twenty hours per week in the school cafeteria, the advancement office, and the local Subway, just a few blocks from my dormitory. I worked only because I had to. Most of my college friends did not work and focused on studying. I was trying to make money to have something to spend and put toward paying my school bills for the following year.

During my junior year, I was talking with Kristen, a resident director at one of the women's dormitories, about the encounter that I had had during my senior year of high school. I was told for the first time that I had been sexually assaulted. I did not like hearing that phrase, because it meant someone had done something really terrible to me. I tried to defend the guy, saying it was my fault and that I was at that apartment to hang out with him, not the others there. She said it did not matter, that I could not have consented at that age in the state of Oregon at that time, so regardless of my actions, the law would see me as a minor and a victim of statutory rape.

Statutory *rape.*

I fought her harder. He didn't rape me. It could have gone further. I was there on my own accord, despite shaking uncontrollably. He didn't tie me up or handcuff me. It didn't matter, she said. In the eyes of the law, sex included many types of sexual contact, which meant rape also included those types of sex. What I had shared with her was legally considered to be sex.

Did that mean I was really a sexual assault victim? How had I not known until now?

I was devastated. I didn't want this to be my story. I didn't want to be a *victim*—and a statutory rape victim, no less. I had finally put enough time between myself and my senior year of high school to have moved on mentally and emotionally by the second half of college. I felt furious with him now. I was beginning to see how he had selfishly taken advantage of the situation for his benefit. It did not matter that I followed him to the car. I was legally classified as a child. He was twenty-one. He knew better.

I now had to consider myself a victim. This changed who I was, learning that I was a victim. Even though it was my secret, I felt that everyone around me knew I was a victim. They could see through my tough exterior.

At the beginning of my junior year in college, I declared journalism as my major.

I had been writing for the *Asbury Collegian* student newspaper during the first semester of my freshman year. The only semester that I did not participate on the paper was during my senior year when I went to Washington for a semester-long internship at the *Washington Examiner*.

Asbury had a requirement that journalism students complete a semester internship in their field, and because I was going to school out of my own pocket and worked full-time during the summer, I chose to intern in Washington during the semester.

The internship placed me at the *Washington Examiner*, where I went on to work full-time years later. I interned for the online desk. It was a difficult internship, and I knew nothing about the media despite wanting to be a journalist. I had not paid much attention to the news while I was in college except for what was going on across our small campus.

My time in Washington in 2010 was overwhelming. I had never been to that city before, and my knowledge of it was embarrassingly limited. I did not know the difference between the White House and the U.S. Capitol. (I cringe to even admit that now.) I once called then-House Speaker John Boehner's office and mispronounced his name in front of his staff and my colleagues. (I will let you guess how I pronounced it.)

I share that because even though I felt that I was born to be a writer, I was a terrible intern with little knowledge of policy, politics, or the media landscape. I just liked to write, but I had focused my writing in high school and college on telling human interest stories or feature pieces. I did not understand what Congress was. Was it the House and the Senate? Just the House?

I left Washington in December 2010, overwhelmed by all that I had experienced that semester and what had been going on back at home in Oregon. My father had resigned from his job in Portland while I was in college, shortly before the 2008–2009 recession. My mother worked full-time at a coffee shop and was laid off when the place closed down. I was on the other side of the country in college through all of this.

After returning to college from Washington, I decided that I did not want to be a journalist and would pursue a different career, though I did not know what it would be.

I graduated in 2011, and I started working two jobs six days a week at a yogurt shop and a clothing store, saving up money to pay off my student loans and to eventually move out of my parents' house. I lived with my parents for almost two and a half years, all the while trying to come up with a plan of what to do next. My future was so wide open that it felt paralyzing.

While back in Oregon after college, I looked up the man from my high school encounter and decided to contact him on Facebook. I asked if he remembered me, and he said he did. I wanted to tell him that what he did was wrong. I was a minor and he was twenty-one when he took me to his car, and he never should have done that to me. I spoke my peace, which he did not receive well. He wrote back that I had asked for it and that he thought I was eighteen.

Despite our disagreement, he asked to meet up, but something in me said, "Stay away, Anna." So I stayed away. I never made plans to see him and blocked him. I had said what I wanted to say to him, but now I was confused again and wondered if this incident years earlier was my fault. So which was it? Was I the victim or the one to blame?

That Facebook exchange in 2011 was the last time we spoke. The statute of limitations passed a few years later. I never wanted or intended to bring a charge against him. I just wanted an apology. I wanted him to say, "I knew you were too young and I should not have done it. I hope you can forgive me."

But that's the problem with life after assault. You want acknowledgment that what happened to you was wrong. You want the person who did it to recognize it. You also want assurance that he is not hurting others and that he is sorry for what he did to you. It is doubly painful to go through sexual assault and believe afterward that your pain is a result of what you did to yourself. That is why sexual assault is so brutal to overcome. You oscillate between believing someone hurt you and that you hurt yourself. Which was it?

Sexual assault teaches you to doubt your judgment and your ability to trust yourself. So there I was, convinced of one thing only to be told I had done this to myself. This left me unable to trust my own judgment.

A few months later, my parents and I moved across the country to North Carolina, and I put that incident behind me.

CHAPTER 2

THE WASHINGTON DAYS

I found a full-time sales job at Ann Taylor in Greensboro, N.C. In the midst of this period being back on the East Coast, I began to think about moving to Washington. I had not enjoyed that city, primarily because I did not understood politics and policy, but I knew more about working in Washington than about writing for a small-town paper. I still was not sure about being a journalist or what politics reporting would be like, but what else would I pursue?

If I stayed in retail, I would regret not having gone after what I went to college for. Not having had a pleasant internship in Washington a year earlier made me want to try harder and prove that I had what it took to be there.

I saved up money and was able to land an internship in Washington in the fall of 2013. I paid $900 a month to share a studio apartment at the Heritage Foundation think tank's intern house on Capitol Hill.

I had no "in" in Washington, unlike those who had family or friends to help them find their way. I had saved a few business cards from professionals I had met three years earlier during my college internship. I reached out to them with nothing to lose.

"Hello, I met you briefly when you spoke at an event … I want to return to Washington… Can you help me?"

I made the move with no back-up plan. I would learn how to report on Capitol Hill or fail trying—and failure was not an option.

That was where the National Journalism Center came in. I learned of a semester-long journalism program that trained entry-level reporters and provided a small stipend to help cover monthly expenses. It was funded by the Young America's Foundation, a conservative organization based outside of Washington that was connected to the Reagan Foundation. I was hesitant about doing a program with a partisan affiliation, but they had a record of successful alumni, so I applied and got in.

NJC placed me at *CQ Roll Call*, an online and print newspaper that covered news on Capitol Hill. I started my internship writing for *CQ Roll Call.* I worked nights at Ann Taylor to make extra cash to help cover costs.

On the final day of that *CQ Roll Call* internship, I got a phone call from a start-up news outlet backed by Cox Media Group called Rare. I landed a full-time internship there. I left them about six months later, after my mentor put a plug in for me with an immigration organization that he said would pay far better than what I was earning at Rare. I knew nothing about immigration, but it seemed to be a great way to learn about the issue and public policy.

I signed on as the Federation for American Immigration Reform's press secretary. The communications director told me that he would do the interviews, and it was my job to book them and collect news clips of immigration news to share with the staff every day. I stayed at FAIR for about a year and a half before choosing to go back into journalism.

In October 2015, in an effort to get back into the media, I took a 4 p.m. to midnight breaking news shift five nights a week at the *Washington Examiner*, where I wrote eight short news stories per shift. It gave me an opportunity to cover all types of stories and see what I enjoyed the most. Was it healthcare? Business? World affairs? Military? Technology?

I was most familiar with immigration and border issues. It was 2016, and the company did not have a reporter who focused on homeland security matters or immigration. Presidential hopeful Donald Trump was then the leading Republican candidate. I began to cover big drug busts by the Border Patrol and immigration raids by ICE. Little did I know that the unlikeliest of candidates would become president and would put a national spotlight on immigration for years to come.

As a reporter for the *Washington Examiner*, I made a case to management that with President Donald Trump in office, we should designate a reporter who focuses on the issue of immigration. Management agreed.

I shifted from breaking news to covering the Department of Homeland Security. I was now a beat reporter for a national news outlet. I could breathe more easily after several years of trying to get my foot in the door.

I became familiar with federal immigration data and was able to recite previous months' statistics from memory. I began attending press briefings at U.S. Customs and Border Protection's headquarters at the Ronald Reagan building near the White House. I began to travel for work, flying down to various parts of the U.S.-Mexico border to tour the international boundary.

Between 2018 and early 2020, I traveled dozens of times for work. I went to the border security expo and conference annually, began to appear on cable news, and spent many evening hours tracking developments on my beat and punching in late at night to grab a breaking story. I also attended countless meetings with sources within the DHS, and I found my place within journalism. I never planned to be a DHS reporter; it just happened. But once it did, it seemed to be where I always belonged.

During my time in Washington, I faced sexual harassment at work. I've chosen not to name the company where it occurred because I see the issue of gender-based harassment and assault as being so much bigger than outing one man or company. This isn't about vilifying a company or person—it's about understanding how pervasive these issues are in America today. I wanted nothing more than to pursue success in Washington and one man saw that as his opportunity.

I did not have a good understanding of what sexual harassment was during my first couple years in Washington—prior to the "MeToo" movement. What I knew about it was what I had seen in movies and in the media. I didn't know any other women who had been sexually harassed on the job or how to respond to it.

So when a superior at my company sent me a text message stating that he had a "proposition" for me, I didn't understand the pitch that he was setting up. I thought he was about to ask to not say anything to his boss if he stepped out of work for a few hours, and he would do the same for me sometime.

I was as naïve as they came.

I share this part of my journey because the person I was when I was assaulted on the street in Washington in 2020 was not someone who had never been a victim of harassment and assault. I was already dealing with past hurt. Yes, you do get over such trauma to some degree; time helps. But it never leaves you. You are never the person you were before an assault. And being reminded of that—by being victim of harassment or a new assault—dredges up the old on top of the new.

With each of the three incidents I went through, I was further crippled. It was only after the third incident that I got the professional help I really needed to address all three incidents, not just the most recent one.

The title of this memoir is as applicable to my experience as a crime reporter who overcame sexual trauma and injustice in 2020 as it is to my experience as an employee who was harassed and pushed into a horrible situation while working in Washington.

I have chosen to withhold the name of the superior at work who propositioned me for sex out of concern for my safety. It is also why I stayed quiet for years. Women who name names face retaliation. Women who don't name names are ridiculed for being too scared, or worse, they are accused of making up the stories. Women who stay silent are mocked for not speaking up. Women cannot win!

A superior at work, fifteen years my senior and married, took what I thought was a professional interest in me. It made me think that he saw something in me and cared about my development as a professional. I was naive, so I did not understand that this was all part of his grooming process.

We had a professional relationship, so when I received a text from him asking for sex, it was a shock. There had been no sexting or flirting or hook-ups before this. I was dead-focused on my job, too ignorant to see who was lurking around at work.

"I have a proposition for you," he wrote in a text message to me.

In writing, he told me his proposition: that if I had sex with him, *it would be good for me*. It would be good for me *how*? Would I get a promotion? Would he have me fired if I said no? If I were to give in, would it be good for me because I would not get fired?

I wanted out of this text exchange, but he would not respect my "no" in text, so he sent me more text messages throughout that day, begging to have sex. This continued for days.

I refused to have sex with him, which he used as a bargaining tool to see what I would be willing to do in return for something that would be "good for" me, as he had previously promised. We never worked out what that "good for you" part of the proposition was, and there was no upside for me at work in the months that followed.

I did not recognize the power dynamic at play. I felt that he was not giving me a choice. He was no longer sending me text messages *asking* for sex; he was *telling* me it was going to happen.

I worried that reporting this to the company would be seen as me making a bigger deal out of something than it was. If the company representative called this superior in to talk, he would probably tell the company that he was kidding, and I would be the one embarrassed for overreacting to his advances.

I did not know until years later that I could (and should) have filed a harassment complaint with the Equal Employment Opportunity Commission (EEOC) or the D.C. Office of Human Rights.

He came over to my apartment one night. I had relented and wanted to get this over with and move on. I had said I would give him something, but not everything.

I hated every minute of what happened that evening, and after he left, I ran to the bathroom and vomited. I felt dirty. I was in my mid-twenties, but in that moment I was right back to being seventeen years old. I hated this man for what he did to me that night and how he saw me. It happened two more times, and after the third time, I finally worked up the courage to say, “No more.”

That was one of the scariest conversations I’ve ever had, but I did it. And he stopped. Only now I was angry with myself for not having stopped it sooner. Had I really had a choice all along?

A few weeks later, he reached out to tell me that he was leaving our company for a new job in Washington.

He has since remarried.

This incident occurred before the “MeToo” movement. It was not until stories of harassment began to come out during that period that I realized that what the superior had manipulated me into was absolutely wrong and was his fault, not mine.

I was reading an article about a news editor at a company in Washington who had used the same proposition line on women reporters.

Only after reading that story did I realize that the position my superior had put me in was the same as the editor in the story. It was easy to see when the situation applied to other women and their superiors that it was coercion. It was not until I saw it from that perspective that I realized my situation was the same as theirs: coercion, abuse of power, and harassment.

I wish I had reached out to lawyers for real support and help, as well as a therapist or counselor.

I was doing so well when this superior propositioned me. After the assault, I gained 70 pounds over the course of a year. I knew that I was upset by what had happened, but I did not realize how upset I was. People around me who did not know what had happened could tell that something had triggered the sudden weight gain.

Without realizing it, I had turned to food at night to stifle the sorrow, the shame, the embarrassment, and the anger that I felt. He took something from me. Another man had taken something from me. I thought what had happened to me at age seventeen was bad enough, and I had made peace with it. Now, I was knocked down again, trying to move forward but unable to fathom why this incident had sidelined me.

I didn't realize how much it had affected me. I stopped dating for a number of years. By early 2020, I was working up the courage to open up to dating again and getting back in shape. And that's when I was assaulted in the street.

Sexual assault kept taking my life from me. It had taken me years to move on from what happened at age seventeen. In Washington, I was thriving when I encountered my superior at work. The way he treated me and showed me how little I was worth destroyed me.

Men don't have any idea what they take from women when they sexually manipulate and abuse them. But women know. They never get it back either as they learn to live a new normal. They grieve for who they were before being harassed and assaulted, because those encounters destroy them on the inside. Even with considerable help from professionals, they are the not the same years later. Even on my best days now—and they are great—I'm not the woman or girl that I was before those attacks. I have grieved fully, although sometimes I still have to face this truth, grieve it, and accept it again.

That is what sexual assault does: it triggers grief. Someone has taken something from you. It does not matter if you were a child, an adult, or elderly. No woman is immune from the impact of sexual assault.

I mentioned at the start of this book that you lose a part of yourself and don't necessarily understand what has changed in you after an assault, but you know that something is very different. That so clearly occurred after the assaults in my teens, twenties, and thirties. You can't solve or fix what you don't understand, making assault recovery that much more mind-bending and aggravating to overcome.

I finally confronted the superior at work. I went on Twitter and sent him the line that he and the editor in the other story had used on their victims. He wrote back and said that I should know the facts before accusing him, and he painted me as the one who caused this to happen in the first place. I had not wanted any of this. I wanted the life I was living before he came into it.

So I steered clear of men and dating. I was at a point in my life where I wanted to be dating, and I hoped to be married by my early thirties. But I couldn't move toward that goal after what happened with the superior. It had taken years to get back to myself, and just as I did, I was taken down again.

CHAPTER 3

THE ATTACK

I was on a work trip to San Antonio, Texas, when my world began to fall apart in mid-March 2020.

President Donald Trump declared a national emergency in March 2020. I was listening to the radio on the way to the San Antonio airport when the host stated that the president had declared a national emergency over the coronavirus pandemic. Not that national emergency declarations happen every day, because they certainly do not, but this one was especially noteworthy.

In January 2020, the House and Senate had begun holding hearings about something called the coronavirus. It was said to be a dangerous illness that was impacting China and could be on the way to the U.S. and the rest of the world. It was believed to be one of the deadliest viruses ever. Little did we know that it was already stateside.

In the two months since January, COVID-19 gained traction in news coverage, particularly within my beat because of the threat to homeland security, including the supply chain and public health. When I had departed Washington in mid-March 2020 for an expo in San Antonio, I was not concerned about going on lockdown. Yet in a matter of days after arriving in Texas, news from the White House had shifted quickly.

I boarded my flight back home to Washington Reagan National Airport on that Friday, March 13, 2020, concerned about the national emergency, but still assuming it would all blow over not long after I returned to my small apartment on Capitol Hill.

The following day, Saturday, I went on a walk along the south side of the National Mall. I was stunned as I saw few people out and about. The lockdown orders were in effect, but I figured that as long as I was walking on the street, not near people, I was not in danger or putting others in danger. Clearly, everyone else was more concerned than I was. It was bizarre to see Washington approaching the biggest tourist event of the year, the Cherry Blossom Festival, without tourists or locals out and about.

The way most of the country experienced the lockdowns cannot compare to how people in major northern cities did, which added to how challenging the recovery from my attack on the street would be.

That weekend, our company instructed employees not to return to the office but to work from home for the time being.

Over the next few weeks, work from home continued. Military deployments meant to enforce social distancing expanded in Washington and other cities around the country.

I remember it well because I covered the developments every day. The National Guard deployed 1,500 personnel in select states to help besieged healthcare workers deal with the influx of coronavirus patients. It was overwhelming to see medical offices and hospitals over capacity. Overflow tents served as morgues. Body bags were in high demand. My own fears began to grow. Maybe COVID-19 really was dangerous. But I was young. I should be fine.

The Air and Army National Guard began working in twenty-two states, including some of those hardest-hit: New York, New Jersey, and Colorado.

"This COVID-19 pandemic is a historic event, and it requires a historic response from the National Guard," Air Force General Joseph Lengyel, the National Guard chief, said in a statement at the time.

Just days after March 15, 2020, approximately 10,000 National Guard personnel were activated across all fifty states, three U.S. territories, and D.C. to assist at drive-through testing sites and to provide food and transportation to those in need.

National Guard personnel across the country were activated on a state-by-state basis to help local law enforcement maintain social distancing and stay-at-home orders among the public.

In Washington, it meant every time I went on an evening walk around my Capitol Hill neighborhood, I would see several armed National Guard soldiers standing around at the park. It was unnerving. It was our new normal, so it was not broadcast on televisions nationwide, but when I share this with people who live in suburban or rural areas of the country, they are stunned that soldiers were out in public to enforce social distancing.

The military did not play down COVID or its response to the virus.

"With COVID-19, it's like we have 54 different hurricanes hitting every state, every territory, and the District of Columbia. Some are Category 5, some are Category 3, and some are Category 1," National Guard chief, General Joseph Lengyel, said in a statement.

Now, two weeks into the pandemic, I was busy reporting from home on the fallout of the pandemic at the border. My news outlet, the *Washington Examiner*, was first to report that the Border Patrol had begun sending back across the border all apprehended illegal immigrants instead of taking them to immigration detention facilities for normal processing.

"The CDC order directs the department to suspend the introduction of all individuals seeking to enter the U.S. without proper travel documentation," acting Homeland Security Secretary Chad Wolf said during a White House press briefing in late March 2020. "That's for both the northern and southern border. The CDC director has determined that the introduction and spread of the coronavirus in the department's Border Patrol stations and detention facilities presents a serious danger to migrants, our front-line agents, our officers, and the American people."

Citizens of more than 120 countries were arrested illegally entering the United States. We knew that COVID-19 was coming from China, but the public (much less the government) could not be sure that it was not also spreading through the southern border. By the same logic, there was also concern that airline passengers coming in and going out of the U.S. also posed a serious threat to all nations, and air travel was halted for months.

All nonessential travel between the U.S. and Mexico and between the U.S. and Canada was also banned at midnight on March 20.

In the days leading up to being attacked on the street on April 4, 2020, I wrote a story about how the U.S. had yet to see civil unrest, but that looting and rioting were possible as the pandemic would set in for the long haul, according to crime, economic, and behavioral experts.

This was my reality: sitting at home, every day, all day, alone, hearing seemingly endless sirens going back and forth outside my window. I spent mornings, afternoons, and evenings working, obsessed over every detail about the pandemic and how society could fall apart. I was not consciously scared for my future or the future of the country or world, but I was not *not* scared. I was already overwhelmed by bad news, and now I was about to face the unthinkable, on top of what was happening around me.

Do you have a worst day, when everything broke—when *you* broke?

Just the thought of it might send you into a panic or cause you to put this book down for a moment. I understand.

We all have one—sometimes more than one.

For me, my very worst day was April 4, 2020.

I had been living my dream. I was a national politics reporter for the *Washington Examiner*, where I focused on homeland security.

I had spent a decade working toward this moment and earning my spot in the national media, specifically in the immigration world. Countless others stood in the imaginary line behind me, all of whom were eager to replace me should I at some point become replaceable.

I was thirty years old and finding my place in Washington. It was my home, and I planned to be there for decades to come. I went to church at Passion City DC on U Street NW, shopped for groceries at Trader Joe's on 14th Street NW, and brunched on the weekends in Georgetown or at Union Market. I had put down roots in my seven years in Washington, and it felt good.

April 4th was a Saturday. It was a party cloudy, chilly day, standard for that time of year in Washington.

I had sold a book on eBay earlier that week. I needed to ship the item to the buyer, so I walked a few blocks to a nearby post office to pay for the hand-labeled envelope. Saturday morning would be the perfect time to run that errand and then return home. With lockdowns in full effect, I was mindful of being out in public and tried to keep my errands to a minimum.

My free time during the lockdowns—now at the end of week three—consisted of binge-watching HGTV, Magnolia Network, Hallmark Channel, and Netflix. I also was getting a little too good at putting together 1,000-piece jigsaw puzzles on my kitchen island while watching TV to pass the time (and taking a break from scrolling news headlines and my Twitter feed).

I would go on a walk every day after work. It was the only time that I left the house with the exception of going to the nearby grocery store once a week or to run an errand. There were no nail appointments, no having a beer at a bar, no walking around the wharf district for fun after dinner. Grocery shopping had become a chore. Shelves were often sold out of key items, and people moved about the store terrified of getting too close to others.

That Saturday morning, I put on my favorite black Nike hoodie and black joggers. I grabbed my keys, iPhone, and manila envelope package and walked out my door. I walked to the elevator, taking it down to the first floor, and walked through the long lobby to the main entrance and exited onto the street, 2nd Avenue NE.

I crossed the one-lane street and walked a few dozen feet in the direction of the post office when I noticed a deranged man wobbling down the sidewalk in my direction. He was about half a block away, then he suddenly diverted from my side of the street into the street and appeared to be going to the other side, drifting like a zombie would stumble around. I was relieved that I would not have to get close to him.

Living next to Union Station and close to an overpass on K Street where homeless people had set up tents, it was not unusual to see someone sleeping on the ground or rows of tents lined up nearby or even people unconscious on the ground, likely due to a drug overdose.

My route to the post office that morning ran along the Securities Exchange Commission property directly next to Union Station, and the post office was housed on the other side of the station.

As I continued walking, I noticed that this man had suddenly shifted back toward my side of the street and onto the sidewalk. He had thrown his chest and face toward a man walking a dog, roughly fifty feet ahead of me. It looked like the man was begging for money and was annoyed that the dog walker had not given him anything. Being approached for money was not out of the ordinary, and there was nothing to fear, even though this man was a little odd.

I had my eyes on this man as he moved past the walker and his dog and toward me. I continued walking in his direction to the end of the block where I would turn right and enter Union Station.

Some say that in a life-or-death situation, time seems to speed up or slow down, or you just sort of exist without realizing you are alive.

I remember closing in on this man as we went from a few dozen feet to ten feet apart. As we got closer to walk past each other on the sidewalk, he leaned toward me as he had with the dog walker. I was not carrying any cash that day, and I also feared getting too close to anyone because of the pandemic. Instinctively, I put my hand up in the air to communicate to him that I did not have money to give him and did not want to interact with him.

That was when he struck.

Suddenly, his arms were around me. I could not escape. This man had me in his clutches. All the while, he screamed as loudly as I had ever heard anyone scream: "THEY'RE TRYING TO KILL ME! THEY'RE TRYING TO KILL ME!" Over and over, he kept shrieking out those words in my ears.

I was in disbelief. What was happening right now? It felt as if I were suspended in time, coming to terms with what was happening and what could come next from him.

I quickly realized that I was helpless. There was no self-defense move that I knew that could get me out of his arms and away from being pressed against his body. He was a large man, towering well over six feet tall. I was 5'4". He was dressed in sweats. He seemed to be having some kind of frantic breakdown. My next move would make or break what happened to me. I was not dealing with a sane man. He was having a serious drug reaction or mental health breakdown—or he was pretending to have one as he assaulted me. I didn't know what his goal was—sex, murder, just lashing out. My decisions in that instant would determine what happened to me.

As he held tightly onto me, I screamed.

I screamed at the top of my lungs in a way that I had not known was possible. It was the one thing that went right in that moment. I was frightened as I heard myself scream like that. I could not hear him over my.blood-curdling scream. If you had been nearby and heard it, you would not have wondered if someone was in trouble. You would have known, without a doubt, that a woman was screaming for her life.

As the attack continued, he fought to get me down to the ground. Some parts of the attack I do not remember as hands and body parts moved to other places, but I do remember the moment he put his hand in my crotch.

That moment I remember clearly. Screaming was my first response. I had been activated to do something. But the crotch grab activated me to fight.

I had one thought in that moment. It was to survive. He had activated a part of me that had been trampled on years earlier when I was assaulted as a teenager and again when I was pushed by a boss to give him what he wanted. This time, I would fight with everything I had to avoid what happened years earlier. I would not be forced into something I did not want. My scream was my "no," and I would fight to the death.

"I am going to kill you!" That was my only thought. Something in me snapped. I'd never felt that intrinsic survival desire before. I was completely activated to save my life and suddenly willing to kill him if he continued this physical and sexual assault.

Something in me had shifted.

I thought about how to fight back. My arms were still pinned down, even though one of his hands was in my crouch. It didn't make sense, but I also couldn't move my head to see our positioning. All I had was my legs. I was scared that if I went on the offensive and tried to hurt him, he could easily hurt me even more. I couldn't lift my head up since it was buried in his chest. I decided my best move would be to lift my right knee and kick him in the groin as hard as I could. Hopefully, he would let go of me, fall over, and I would have a chance to get away.

I forcefully lifted my right knee.

The next moment, I was looking over my right shoulder and he was thirty feet away, limping away in the same awkward way that he had approached me. It was over. But what had just happened?

The part I don't remember is how he got off me or got away.

I watched him limp away as my surroundings came back into focus. It seemed that I had zoned out or had gone to sleep with my eyes open. I felt as though I had been knocked unconscious and could not remember where I was or what had just happened. My ears were ringing loudly.

A woman was standing near me, asking if I was OK. A man was also there. I could not think of what to say to them as I was trying to catch my breath. It seemed that everything around me was spinning, but everyone else seemed fine. I tried to speak a few times before I could finally get words out of my mouth. I told the woman, "9-1-1. Call 9-1-1." Then I thought about it. Was this an emergency? I was genuinely confused as to whether calling 9-1-1 was appropriate. I still could not put into words what had just happened. I didn't register that it was an assault. It felt as if I had just woken up after surgery and could not remember where I was or the circumstances that led me there.

But something in me said, "Call 9-1-1."

The woman began to make the call, and I tried to find my phone. I don't remember if it was in my pocket, in my hand, or on the ground, but when I found it, I began to call for help as well.

The man standing nearby told me that he had run across the street from a construction site when he heard the screaming. His name was Donny. He said he had gotten my attacker off and away from me.

I remembered now. There had been a lot of screaming. I remembered screaming and hearing the attacker scream. Details were piecing themselves together in my head, albeit slowly.

It doesn't occur to you when you're in the middle of something traumatic that you're in the middle of something traumatic. You don't think, "This is a traumatic event."

We made our calls to 9-1-1, and I got my bearings. Parts of the attack started to auto-populate in my head as those standing around talked about what they had seen and heard. I realized that I was still holding the envelope, which was now crumpled up. It was a clue that I had been doing something. I had been walking to the post office. "Oh yes, the eBay item. I was shipping it."

Other onlookers farther away were coming over from across the street and down the block to help. The only person who didn't make any effort to help was the man who had been walking the dog some distance in front of me. I remember seeing him with his headphones in his ears when he first went by me. He apparently was oblivious to the commotion.

The police officers began showing up, one by one, in their squad cars. I heard the sirens before I saw them. Hearing those sirens was energizing, like hope was on its way. I felt safer knowing they were coming to help me. I would certainly be safe now. That man couldn't come back while they were there. Or if he did, he would not get to me.

The police marked off two blocks of the sidewalk, but people ignored the tape and continued to walk through the scene. Police were overwhelmed trying to block off the area while also separating me from witnesses to get their statements. Enforcing the police tape zone was not their top priority, and as a result, the scene became contaminated, making it impossible for the K9 unit that would come through to track the suspect's scent on the ground after he fled.

They asked me to recount what had happened, and I shared what I'd experienced. I mentioned that the man put his hand in my crotch and that all I remembered next was his running away, and that it was blurry and overwhelming. Suddenly, the mood of the investigation shifted. Immediately, the police officer pulled away from me and asked me to excuse him. I heard him get on his radio and call for backup from the Sexual Assault Response Team.

I suddenly realized why he had stepped away: I had stated that it was a sex crime without actually saying "sex crime" or "sexual assault." I had not realized that when I told the officer where the man stuck his hand, the officer immediately realized this was not just a physical assault. The officer said a K9 officer would be coming on site to attempt to track down the man based on the scent off of my clothes and the ground where the assault took place.

Pedestrians continued to walk through the taped-off area. The K9 was delayed until a sergeant from the sexual assault unit could arrive on scene. Without the dog and with people continuing to taint the area, it was becoming less likely the dog would be able to track down the suspect.

I discovered that there is a lot of waiting when it comes to police taking a report. A lot of what you don't see in crime shows on TV is the standing around.

Finally, another police vehicle pulled up. The driver got out of the car and spoke with the other officers on the scene. One officer turned and motioned toward me. He came over and introduced himself as a detective from the sexual assault unit and asked if we could speak somewhere private and quiet.

The detective escorted me over to his car, and I got in the front seat. I realized as I sat there that my arms, upper body, legs, and head were shaking uncontrollably. The detective was not particularly consoling or understanding; he was just there to ask questions. All I wanted was someone to physically hold me (ironically) and tell me I was OK, even though I was not. The more police that showed up, the more I felt that this was a big deal, and I didn't want a big deal. Just take my report, find the guy, and let's move on. This was beginning to feel overwhelming.

The detective would ask a question, and then sounds of drilling from the construction site directly across the street from the SEC building would start again, drowning out what I was trying to say. We constantly had to pause for the drilling to stop so we could hear each other.

At the end of our conversation, he asked if I would provide my clothing, a sweatshirt and pants, for DNA purposes. If the attacker had a criminal history, any DNA that he left on my clothes would match what was already in the system. I was still holding out hope that police would find the man that day. If they didn't, this would be the only way to know who he was and have any hope of tracking him down. If we did not get a DNA match and he was not caught, we would likely never catch him or know who he was.

All of this was a shock to me. Less than an hour earlier, I had been walking to the post office. I simply wanted to mail a package, and here I was sitting in a police car. I was being told that I would potentially be the plaintiff in a federal trial because felonies in Washington were prosecuted by the U.S. Attorney's Office, not a county district attorney. I did not understand what was happening. Nobody even knew who had attacked me, but if he was found, we were going to trial at the federal level. Even in my shock, that part grabbed my attention.

Because of the construction site noise outside, giving my statement took some time. I grew inpatient as I wanted to get out of the car and go to the post office and finish what I had started. The more that my memory of the attack came back to me, the more I wanted to move on from this. I just wanted to go mail my package. It was hanging over me.

An ambulance and first responders then looked me over. They encouraged me to go to the hospital and get tests done to ensure nothing was broken. I didn't feel any physical pain, but I was still too much in the moment to have recognized it. I declined the ambulance to the hospital.

The police escorted me on foot one block back to my apartment building, Station House, and waited in the building lobby while I walked back up to my apartment and changed my clothes.

CHAPTER 4

THE AFTERMATH

I got up to my apartment and walked inside. The cat was there looking at me. I took off my clothes and realized again that I was still shaking. I was also freezing as I stood there naked. I realized I had forgotten what I was doing. How long had I just been standing there zoned out?

As I undressed, I was forced to think about why I was undressing—because someone had just hurt me. Why did he attack me? I didn't even look appealing that day on the street. I had been minding my own business. I didn't start anything.

I could still feel his hand in my crotch. Ugh. It was disgusting. I hated that feeling. I cringed. I wanted that feeling and memory to be gone. I put on a new pair of underwear and a new outfit. I was still living in the adrenaline of it all and could not calm down. But I had more important problems than getting my body to stop shaking at this moment. I wanted the feeling of his hand GONE.

I was enraged and felt like screaming furiously again, but instead I let out a soft cry, more like a whimper. I felt bad for keeping the officers waiting as I cried quietly in my bedroom for a few minutes. I needed to get back downstairs.

I went downstairs and handed the clothes off to the detective and officer. One said it could take up to eight weeks before they got a hit in the system, if he was already in the system.

The officer asked if I would like the clothes back after the DNA process was completed.

"Are you kidding me?" I thought. I shook my head. I never wanted to see that outfit again. I never wanted any of this.

I would now face six to eight weeks of living in my apartment, wondering if the man purposely targeted me for the attack. Had he been following me for weeks or months? Had I not been paying attention? Was he an angry reader, upset about what I had reported? Had he sent me a threatening email that had gone to spam, which I had not noticed, and now he was out for revenge? Was he a lunatic who lunged at me because of how I dressed or looked? Was this a racial attack based on the ethnicity he thought I was? Was he planning to come after me again the next time I walked outside my apartment building? Should I start getting my groceries delivered to the apartment building?

Since the police said that they had no idea who he was, I had only my memory to recall what he looked like. Because of the nature of the attack and my only focus being on surviving, all I could remember was that he was a large Black man between about thirty-five and fifty years old. He had been wearing sweatpants and a zip-up sweatshirt.

But what if he changed clothes? Would I recognize him in a different outfit? What if he was homeless and lived nearby? Had I walked by him before and never noticed him? Had he previously asked for money and I had ignored him? These were all questions that the police could not answer for me, and when they left that day, they left me helpless.

I did not own a gun. My only tool for self-defense—my intuition—had been shattered that day. I had not seen the attack coming, and I had always relied on my seemingly innate sense of street smarts to protect myself. I felt as though I could not trust myself to protect myself.

The only weapon I owned that I could carry with me going forward was a large knife that a U.S. Immigration and Customs Enforcement agent had previously given to me during a trip to the southern border. I had been out to dinner with several of ICE's investigative agents when I told them my plans to drive roughly 400 miles on a back road along the West Texas border the following day.

One of the agents asked if I had a gun to protect myself in case I had car trouble, given the proximity to where the Mexican cartels ran back and forth across the border. I said that I did not have a gun. He pulled out a large folded black knife and gave it to me to protect myself.

I did not even have the knife with me that day when I was attacked. It had been sitting in a drawer in my kitchen in case I went somewhere dangerous and needed it.

Little did I know that walking to the post office was dangerous enough to warrant carrying the knife with me. Even if I'd had that knife, I wouldn't have trusted myself to use it successfully. It was large and hard to hold in my small hand. I also was not convinced that the knife would not have been turned on me if I tried to use it.

My mind was overwhelmed by my thoughts. I was sitting in my apartment, unsure of what to do next. I looked down and realized that I had picked my package back up and was holding it again.

Do I just go back to living my life as though nothing has changed?

Was I supposed to just do a load of laundry and then take a nap and make an early dinner afterward? I was in disbelief about what had happened. I had never felt so overwhelmed.

I lay down on the floor in my bedroom and on my bed for hours on the afternoon of the attack. I tried to take a nap at one point, and I clearly remember what I saw as I closed my eyes. It was a blank background with circular lines drawn in every direction coming out of the corners and edges of the screen. My mind looked like the static channel on an old TV screen. There was no continuity or sense to what I was seeing when I closed my eyes other than it really spoke to the confusion and state of being overwhelmed.

That visual scared me as I was trying to drift off to sleep because I felt no mental rest. It's one thing to be stressed and have a hard time relaxing, but it's another to be hurt in the way that I was in the attack and try to rest afterward. I found that my mind and body could not rest. Instead, I felt I'd been catapulted into the air and didn't know when the free fall would end.

I felt led to reach out to women in my church. I was part of a chat group through a phone app that had 200 women in it, mostly in their twenties and thirties. All were volunteers at our church. No men were in the group. Most of the women also lived in Washington, and the others lived in the surrounding areas in Maryland and Virginia. I posted in the chat that I had just been assaulted on the street. I said I did not know what to ask for from them, but I needed their prayers. It was a cry for help. What I really wanted was someone to sit with me that day until I was OK being alone again.

In the hours that followed, more than seventy women privately messaged me and commented on my post to say that they were praying for me. I felt their prayers and their interceding on my behalf with God. I believe their prayers mattered that day. It gave me hope and support.

Some in the group sent me a gift card to get some new clothes, knowing that mine had been taken by the police for DNA testing.

One of the volunteer coordinators at church offered to come alongside me. In the weeks that followed, we broke the quarantine rules and got together to go on several walks outside so I did not have to be alone. She knew I physically needed to be around someone. I remember little about our conversations, but what mattered was her willingness to see me in person.

A couple of other girls who I met through the group chat also included me on walks or hung out outside while we were standing six feet apart. I look back at it now and hate that we let a pandemic keep us from hugging and being together. I believe the body needs physical touch from loved ones to know it is loved and to heal.

Unfortunately, while hanging out with some girls, I began to feel more alone than comforted by them. I remember feeling that when a few of us got together near the Capitol. They would talk about their frustrations at work or the monotony of being locked down and unable to do the normal fun things of life. I felt forgotten while sitting next to them. They had no idea what I had been through a few weeks earlier. They were trying to be supportive and inclusive.

But I could not relate to their problems. At one point, some of them began to share their own stories of being sexually assaulted or of others they knew who had been. It was meant to show that they had gotten through it and that I would as well. But I felt they were belittling all the pain and sorrow that I was carrying. I was too scared to share what I was really thinking and feeling, that if I did so, they would think I was a jerk. It was not long after that I decided to drive down to stay with my parents.

I was too proud to ask for people to bring me food or to send me gift cards for delivered meals, I was too tired and helpless to cook for myself. Money was disappearing as I was always ordering out to make sure I was still eating something each day.

So much of my recovery was hampered by the pandemic. I could not see my coworkers, go to the shopping mall, walk to Starbucks, go out with friends for happy hour, go to church and be around people who shared the same foundational spiritual beliefs that I had. I didn't know what I wanted. I wanted to be alone, but I also longed for community and in-person support. I was so fragile and yet incredibly on edge.

Going through the attack in a better point in time—namely, not during a pandemic—would have made a world of difference in my recovery. But I did not have a choice about the point in history that I was attacked, which made it so much worse. It created the perfect storm for me, a crime victim, not to have the community and means to recover.

One thing that I did not do that first day was call my family. I routinely called my parents daily, and it had been that way for years. I always called while walking or while sitting at home or on the bus.

But this time, I did not want to hear from them. I was the one in my family who others teased for having bad luck and having bad things happen. My family joked about it, how I had been bit by a tick, been hit by a cab, gotten a head injury working at Ann Taylor, and gotten a concussion in my office. I did not want to feel belittled and made light of in the midst of what I was facing in that moment. I was scared that if I shared what happened, they would say, "Oh, well, he did not rape you, and you're alive. You're OK! You got away!" I would rather be silent than feel belittled and told to get over it.

All of my injuries since living in Washington were events that my family used to say things along the lines of, "Anna, you have the worst luck, and you will continue to end up in an Emergency Room." In fact, when the ambulance came after the attack, I chose not to go to the hospital to see if I had any injuries because I could hear my family already making light of it: "Oh, Anna, got hauled off in an ambulance today. Big surprise."

I went more than twenty-four hours before I told my family that I had been attacked. The first person I told was my sister. She was upset about what had happened. She did not say anything insensitive, which made me feel better about telling my parents next.

I then told my parents, who were stunned. But it seemed that they were more upset that I had not told them about the attack right after it happened than by the attack itself. It felt as if they were making this about them, not about me.

My parents did not offer to drive the five-hour trip to Washington to be with me because of the pandemic and travel restrictions. But again, to me, it felt like another blow. A man had assaulted me on the street, and they did not make an effort to be with me or to bring me back to North Carolina. Flying seemed out of the question, and I did not have a car. I was stuck.

Unfortunately, this is something that most people do not understand when they are dealing with someone who has just been through a traumatic event. You cannot ask them *if* they are OK. They are *not* OK. But they may *think* they are OK. It is on the family and friends to take action and *not* wait to be asked for help.

It is hard to share this publicly because it is between my family and me. I share it because inevitably someone reading this will be in my family's position. You will find out someone you love has just gone through something horrible. Remember this: they need you. Don't ask *if* they need help. They *need* you, and they *need* help. You just go. Better to make an effort and be rejected than to make none and be wanted.

So many times in the days and weeks after the attack, I should have gone to the hospital for professional care because I could barely take care of myself. I also did not realize how seriously depressed I was.

I had been so independent and relied on myself to do everything that when I ultimately needed help, I still relied on myself to make decisions. But all I really wanted was for someone to come alongside me and support me, even if that meant taking me to the hospital because I was too exhausted to take myself there. Countless times after the attack while I was still in Washington and after I got to my parents' house, intrusive thoughts filling my head scared me and I wanted to call 9-1-1. But I was even more scared of being taken away by an ambulance and put into a psych ward. I thought I might lose my job and everything I had. How would I get released after going to a hospital for suicidal thoughts and ideation? I felt that going there would make me worse because I would not know anyone or my surroundings, and I would be around people going through their own breakdown.

I shared these concerns with my therapist, but looking back, I believe I held so much back from her. I did not want her to force me into a hospital for an evaluation. So I tried to contain the nightmare inside my head on my own.

The mental suffering continued on and off for about two years after the attack. I never thought in high school when they told us about the prevalence of sexual assault that anything could be worse than being physically hurt or raped. But this mental hell was so much worse than physically being hurt.

I was like a zombie living in my body with nothing going on in my head except terrifying thoughts and clinical depression. It had come on slowly after the attack. And then suddenly, in late April, it took me down overnight.

I felt abandoned by God, even though I knew deep down that He was there. He seemed to be hiding from me. I would scream at Him in my bedroom. I asked Him why He would let this happen to me.

I wrestled with God for weeks, and I would continue to in the months that followed. How was this part of His plan for me?

Lying on the floor in my bedroom on the afternoon of April 4, 2020, I was sitting against the side of my bed when it struck me.

This attack, just hours ago, was thirteen years to the week since I was assaulted as a seventeen-year-old.

I was in disbelief.

"Am I cursed?" I wondered.

"I am," I decided. There seemed no reason to argue the other side. "I'm damned. Bad things happen only to me."

As I sat in shock in my silent apartment, I did not believe that this could be a coincidence. I had been assaulted thirteen years apart, in the same week.

The tragedy of the attack this time around was not only in what happened—and that seemed bad enough. I survived what I perceived as a fight for my life and was sexually assaulted in the process. It was in the symbolism of what it meant.

For years, I had lived a story in my head of "Bad things happen to me. I have bad luck. I don't deserve good things. I am unworthy of love. I am scorned." This attack confirmed it.

It was as if no matter what I did in life, no matter how hard I tried, I would never overcome this bad luck. I would never get past the doom that hovered over me in April.

This attack felt like the last nail in my coffin, and this time it had been sealed shut.

Yes, I had survived, for what purpose? To know my future would be miserable? Bad luck and doom awaited me? Was it just me, or did other women experience so many instances of sexual harassment and assault?

In the days and weeks after, I began to believe that I really was doomed. Bad things were always waiting for me. Just as I was doing well, something terrible happened to me.

April 4, 2020, was not the worst day of my life because it was the day that I was attacked on the street and sexually assaulted. It was, at that time and for a number of years that followed, the worst day of my life because it was when I confirmed the deep-seated belief that I had held in my mind since a teenager—that bad things were bound to happen to me.

I was doomed to be a victim.

I was doomed to be single.

I was doomed to have bad luck.

I no longer wondered if I was doomed; I now had the proof to confirm it.

Bad things happened to me and only me. Even those closest to me would joke about it. This attack confirmed it. I should prepare for a life of unpleasantness because just as I was getting along fine, something bad would happen.

I also began to fear how I would stay in Washington when this man was out on the loose. How could I go back to the new normal that I had created for myself during the pandemic's first few weeks? I was now a crime victim. I did not want to be a victim again!

I had been on my way up in my career. I was doing interviews on television news stations, namely Fox News and Fox Business Network, to discuss the state of the southern border. I was finally getting the break that I always wanted and believed that I deserved. All other immigration reporters were from large left-leaning outlets, and I was the only one from a right-leaning paper taking this issue on in 2019. I was starting to make a name for myself.

All of the attention I received from speaking as a right-leaning reporter on immigration would put me on the radar of other news outlets. I had connections with sources in the Trump administration. I had been on a dozen border trips by 2020—something very few of my peers had actually done.

As quickly as my flame was starting to shine, it went out. I was taken down, literally and symbolically, that day.

It was not just me, a thirty-year-old woman, who was assaulted that day.

It was the twenty-something young professional who was manipulated into it.

It was seventeen-year-old me who was assaulted by a twenty-one-year-old man.

How many more times would I have to feel this way?

CHAPTER 5

THE INITIAL RECOVERY

In the initial days after the attack, I had an appointment scheduled with an ear, nose and throat doctor in Arlington, Virginia. I took the train there, determined to continue living life as though nothing had happened.

After the appointment, I walked home from the Ballston Metro neighborhood. It was a seven-mile walk.

I look back now and think how jaded I was. I was paranoid like crazy when I was outside, yet I was simultaneously fixated with proving to myself that everything was fine.

So I walked block after block through Arlington, across the Potomac River, and down to the Lincoln Memorial where I took pictures of ducks wading through the water while I sat at the edge. All the noise in my head quieted down. I then walked down the National Mall and over toward my home at Station House Apartments, right past where the attack had occurred.

I remember being on the walk when my editor called to check in and tell me that I should take time off to relax.

I did not want to relax. I wanted to keep working to stay busy. I was already forced to stay home because of the pandemic. I lived alone and had no one around, and I was six floors above a busy street. I could not bear to sit at home bored all day on top of that. But he insisted, saying, "Take a week off."

I did it begrudgingly, because I knew deep down that my mind needed time to relax. I was also scared to relax and be alone with my thoughts. I could not go out and do normal stuff. We were still at the beginning of COVID. Everything was closed. There was no normal life. There were National Guard soldiers at our parks keeping people six feet apart. All museums were closed. Restaurants were closed. Churches were closed. So I sat at home and did puzzles and watched endless hours of TV and movies.

Then I went back to work. I felt that I was over the attack. I had taken time off and rested.

The immediate realization that I had survived the attack that day and in the days afterward was one that brought gratitude that I was OK.

But my mind did not seem in agreement with my body, which was glad to be OK overall minus bruises and soreness. I was beginning to wonder more about the attack itself in an existential way. Why had it happened? Why in April? Am I really bound to be hurt over and over again? Those thoughts were innumerable and begin to pop into my head repeatedly. I would try to solve them, only to have them pop up again in a new way that I couldn't solve. The more I tried to quiet my mind, the more my mind threw additional questions at me.

I spent my days working and reading horrible headlines. Crime seemed to be everywhere. Sickness and death were rampant. Civil unrest was growing. Nowhere felt safe. My mind jumped back and forth from being convinced the outside was safe to being paranoid that if I left my building, I would be attacked in a new way because that was just my luck—and a crazed man was still out on the loose. What if he was looking for me?

I was also growing frustrated with how I handled the attack. I fought to survive, but I ended up freezing and then finally fighting and then blacking out. Why hadn't I fought back earlier and harder?

I felt ashamed. The question of why I hadn't fought back kept popping up in my mind for months. When I saw the man coming toward me, I did not try to run, I did not kick him in the groin, and I did not take any other offensive or defensive action. I let him put his arms around me. That is why I felt that I had let him hurt me.

Once the attack began, I instinctively screamed. Unlike many dreams that we've all had in which we try to scream but can't, I was able to scream during the attack. I was relieved in that moment that my voice could be heard.

In the weeks after the attack, I began to see a therapist, Susanne. She explained the principle of fight, flight, or freeze. When faced with danger, people will have one of three responses: to take physical action, to shut down and stay, or to try to escape the situation.

In my case, Susanne said that I froze, but I also fought in the only way that I knew how. I initially chose to scream over his screaming, and my screams were louder and of a much higher pitch than his. My shrill screams drew the attention of others on the street, and ultimately people came to help me. I had to face what my response was that day and find a way to accept it. Even though I now had plenty of ideas for how I could have physically fought him, I had to accept that I had done the right thing for me in that moment.

I was eventually able to accept that although I had not kicked him in the groin or bit him or something else, I had done the right thing for me. I had protected myself in the best way that I knew how. But it was hard to arrive at that conclusion for several months.

Some well-meaning friends and family asked why I let this man on the street ambush me and why I didn't fight back. When I was asked these questions, I could shutdown or get raging mad. It seemed that I was being judged for not doing better, as if I were happy about how I had responded. Just as I would begin to accept that I did the right thing for myself that day, someone would ask why I froze.

Not fighting back does not mean that I was OK with what was happening.

What people who have not been in a life-or-death situation, even a sexual assault, may not understand is that you can plan all you want for how to handle dangerous situations—and you should—but your body and mind take over once you are in one.

You are trying to make judgments on what the next move is based on what you have seen and heard leading up to that moment. You are taking into consideration what you have noticed about your attacker—his or her physical strength, size, state of mind, and objective in attacking you. You are not consciously thinking about these things, but your brain instinctively takes all of the information it has and is processing it with lightning speed to come up with your best response.

At the same time, your body may respond differently. My body froze. My mind was taking everything about him and my surroundings into consideration, but my body did not automatically fight back or try to get away. It was not activated to fight until the attack became sexual.

When I would think back to the attack, it felt as if I were right back in it. My heart would race and I would begin to hyperventilate and then panic and cry. It was traumatizing. I did not cry or panic during the attack. That is quintessentially what trauma is—going through a situation that is so taxing that you are unable to react emotionally because you are 100 percent focused on surviving.

The problem was that in reliving the attack, as much as I wanted to go back mentally and consider how I could have handled it better, I was keeping that horror in my head when I really needed to move on.

In therapy, Susanne suggested we try Eye Movement Desensitization and Reprocessing therapy, known as EMDR.

The Cleveland Clinic (https://my.clevelandclinic.org/) defines EMDR as a method that "treats mental health conditions that happen because of memories from traumatic events in your past. It's best known for its role in treating post-traumatic stress disorder (PTSD)."

I was also having trouble walking outside and seeing people who reminded me of the man who attacked me. Any Black men who were taller than six feet and dressed in sweatpants immediately sent me into a panic. Walking a couple of blocks to the grocery store, or on a leisurely walk, it was common to see men who fit that description. It was easier to stay home and isolate than to go outside and be on guard.

This was not like a moment of panic when, for instance, you walk by a parking garage exit and a driver hits his brakes before pulling out as you pass by, causing you to jump. But after 30 seconds, you are fine and have moved on.

This panic sets in when you see someone who you believe is the person who hurt you, Even though you are not being attacked, part of your mind overrules that and says it's time to freeze, flee, or fight. We have heard about the impact of PTSD on military and veterans, but this condition can affect anyone who has been through trauma. If left untreated, it can disrupt your life for months, years, or decades.

Knowing that something was wrong with my mind and that I could not calm down when I saw anyone in public who remotely resembled the man who hurt me, I sought to address it in therapy.

Nonprofit Rape, Abuse & Incest National Network (RAINN) (https://rainn.org/) reports that 70 percent of rape or sexual assault victims experience moderate to severe distress, a larger percentage than for any other violent crime.

A whopping 94 percent of women who are raped experience symptoms of PTSD during the two weeks following an assault.

One-third of women who are raped contemplate suicide. Thirteen percent of women who are raped attempt suicide.

In addition, after sexual assault, survivors are ten times more likely to use illicit drugs.

I learned that in situations like the one that I had been through, the brain's processing system becomes overwhelmed. Integrative Psychotherapy Toronto (https://www.integrativepsychotherapytoronto.com/) explains that the amygdala's "fight-or-flight" response may take over, overwhelming the brain with stress hormones, such as cortisol and adrenaline.

"This response pulls energy away from the prefrontal cortex and hippocampus, which are critical for logical thinking and contextualizing experiences," the Integrative Psychotherapy Toronto website states. "As a result, traumatic memories are stored in their raw, unprocessed form in the amygdala, rather than being integrated into long-term memory. The memory of the event remains vivid and highly emotional, causing individuals to relive the trauma repeatedly. In essence, these memories become 'stuck,' as the brain is unable to reclassify them as past experiences. This phenomenon explains why a certain sight, sound, or situation can instantly trigger intense distress even years after the traumatic event."

The Cleveland Clinic website explains why EMDR is an effective therapy from treating trauma: "Trauma is like a wound that your brain hasn't been allowed to heal. Because it didn't have the chance to heal, your brain didn't receive the message that the danger is over. Newer experiences can link up to earlier trauma experiences and reinforce a negative experience over and over again. That disrupts the links between your senses and memories. And just like your body is sensitive to pain from an injury, your mind has a higher sensitivity to things you saw, heard, smelled or felt during a trauma-related event."

Susanne led me through EMDR by having me close my eyes and go back into that moment while tapping with my hands softly on either side of my head, near my shoulder bone. She led me through every moment of the attack, and I relived all the details. I chose how to feel as I imagined being back in it. I began to see that I really did have very limited options in responding to my attacker and that my brain had done an incredible job in sizing up the situation and causing me to freeze. It took quite a few sessions of EMDR to address the attack and reprocess it.

A British charity organization that works to educate the public about PTSD and EMDR and related treatments, PTSD UK (https://www.ptsduk.org/), explains that while being treated, patients will focus on the troubling memories that they have about themselves related to those memories: "(For example, in dealing with a rape, the person may believe 'I am dirty'). The individual then formulates a positive belief that he would like to have about himself ('I am a worthwhile and good person in control of my life.'). All the physical sensations and emotions that accompany the memory are identified. The individual then goes over the memory while focusing on an external stimulus that creates bilateral (side to side) eye movement. … This process continues until the memory is no longer disturbing,"

PTSD UK also states on its website: "It is believed that EMDR works because the 'bilateral stimulation' by-passes the area of the brain that has become stuck due to the trauma and is preventing the left side of the brain from self-soothing the right side of the brain. During this procedure, clients tend to 'process' the memory in a way that leads to a peaceful resolution. This often results in increased insight regarding both previously disturbing events and long-held negative thoughts about the self that have grown out of the original traumatic event."

The downside was that because unresolved trauma was floating around in my mind between therapy sessions, the panic attacks got worse.

My doctor had put me on a benzodiazepine and several other medications following the attack, but I was scared to take the benzodiazepine pills because I knew they could be addictive.

But after taking the first pill, I realized how much of a game changer it was. Frankly, I wanted to *live* on that medication. I felt normal and sane for the first time in weeks. Although it took a good half-hour or so for one pill to kick in, it could stop a panic attack in its tracks. Sometimes one pill was not enough; I needed two to feel calm. It was incredible how they helped. It was also scary to depend on something to stabilize me rather than be able to control my own mind and body.

If you had asked me in the days after the attack to think back to it, I would have wanted to think about it without my heart rate increasing, my breathing becoming more hurried, and my upper chest lifting itself slightly as my fight, flight, or freeze reaction was triggered.

That is what trauma does. Even weeks after the attack, I was scared to think back to it yet obsessed with reliving it and trying to figure out how I could have avoided it. I was still trying to figure out what went wrong in that moment. Why did I freeze instead of fight? How did he end up getting in my face so quickly, and why didn't I even think to move away before it happened? What if I had taken a different route to the post office?

These types of thoughts were the norm for me, not the exception. They came all times of day and night. It was like running into a brick wall over and over again. Yet I kept forcing myself to run into that wall as if doing so one more time would give me the answers that I was so desperate to unearth.

I knew I was not doing well. I had started to have panic attacks. They were not world-ending, but they were enough to freak me out. They were occurring every few days after years of experiencing them only occasionally.

When I went back to work in mid-April, I was assigned to cover civil unrest in the United States.

The news climate that I walked back into was bleak. The news that I was assigned to cover was the opposite of what I needed to be exposed to on a daily basis if I were going to keep my head in a sound place and avoid anxiety.

I really believed I was fine. I had been through a bizarre attack on the street that I did not entirely remember and survived. I had been sexually abused in public, but I sort of shrugged it off since I'd been through terrible sexual encounters before. I thought that maybe if I downplayed it, I could move on more easily. I really tried to get myself to believe that it was not a big deal, but something in me refused to accept it.

In my mind, I did not want to face the incident. While part of me wanted to figure out why the attack happened, why I was targeted, how I could have fought back or avoided it, and more, I also wanted to move on and not think about it. I was torn between obsessing and avoiding.

I needed good news. What I got was disaster on top of tragedy followed by chaos and civil unrest. The terrifying headlines I saw were starting to scare me, and I was worried about the impact they were having on me. Given what I had just experienced in the assault and the legal saga that was only getting started, having to report on these events could potentially reinforce my fears and germinate new ones. But that was my job; I couldn't quit. I couldn't take endless time off and wait for the pandemic to end. I didn't know when my mind would be in a better place, so I couldn't wait it out.

The stories I wrote on a daily basis in March, April, and May focused on serious crimes committed by gang members, coronavirus deaths and the public's fear of dying from it, and the mass release of jail inmates nationwide.

The shift from general homeland security to covering scarier stories was due to the significant impact of the pandemic on

Americans. Our readers did not want to read immigration news—they wanted to read about the pandemic. It seemed that they wanted to be scared.

I expressed this to my doctor, who I was seeing more because of my increasing anxiety and depression. She told me to take the medicine she had given me and to not be afraid of getting addicted, that it was there to help me. I was still reluctant to use it, even after trying it and taking it here and there during those first few weeks. But I thought about taking it throughout the day.

It was all becoming too much; the news and the panic attacks were overwhelming.

One night on April 28, I woke up at 3 A.M. struggling to breathe and in the middle of a panic attack, only this time I was not merely *worried* that I was dying based on my physical symptoms. I was *convinced* that I was dying.

I called my mom and told her what was happening. I said to her, "I'm dying. It's happening." I knew she was scared because she had never heard me talk like this before.

After talking with her for a few minutes, I was not getting any calmer. I was becoming more hysterical. I cannot put into words how I felt in those minutes. It lasted all night and into the morning and midday. It felt as though I had been separated from my mind and body and was witnessing myself die from the outside. I had no control. Despite feeling that I was on the brink of dropping dead, I continued to live. But whenever I experienced a panic attack, I could not make these connections or recognize such details. And that one was the most intense one I had experienced.

At 11 A.M., I went on a walk and started to calm down. I decided it was not safe for me to be alone. I either needed to go to a hospital or go to my parents' home. I chose the second option. I would rent a car, leave Washington, and go visit my parents for a week to recover there. I looked online at rental cars and found one a few miles away from Union Station. I caught an Uber to the Enterprise location, picked up the car, and drove it back to my apartment. The next morning, I loaded up the cat and some of my belongings, and I began the drive to North Carolina.

I had made the drive down to my parents before and always took the highways. Now, not in my not right mind and acting in survival mode, I took side roads. The trip felt like a never-ending journey through the woods because my backroads route was adding a lot of time.

I had taken a high dose of a benzodiazepine and a depressant before leaving Washington as it was the only way to keep me stable amid the sleep deprivation and panic. It was either go to the hospital or take a high dose of medicine and drive in a sedated state to my family. I could not think clearly as I drove, and my eyes felt heavy. I had recently stopped drinking caffeine because it made the anxiety and panic worse. Somehow I made that drive back home and arrived without incident.

When I finally made it to North Carolina, I stopped at a grocery store to pick up flowers for my parents. Despite all of the stress I was under, I felt that I should arrive with a gift in hand. It is hilarious to think about now because the drive back to my parents was six hours. I was not in my right mind. I now believe that I should not have been driving. The whole trip felt like a long hallucination. I had driven for many hours on one-lane back-country roads in a daze.

Yet when I finally pulled into town, it seemed that I awoke from the daze. I was suddenly in my normal frame of mind as I saw familiar buildings. I parked at a grocery store and walked inside. To my surprise, there was no line, and no security officer was holding people outside the store as there had been at some stores in Washington. I walked in leisurely without anyone telling me to get in line.

What I saw shocked me. I found grocery shelves stocked with food, an abundance of toilet paper, and people shopping as normal, some in face masks and others not. Music was playing over the loudspeakers, and it seemed to be a normal day. I walked over to the flower arrangements. I remember thinking how odd it was that now my biggest concern was picking out flowers when just the day before, I thought I was going to die, and I was confined to my apartment in the city. It was as though I had been jolted from one reality to another.

I bought the flowers and drove to my parents' apartment. I walked in, greeting them with hugs and kisses, and we sat down to dinner.

As we began to eat in front of the television, I felt that familiar, dreaded feeling in my chest, as though it had just dropped into my back. My head began to spin as I felt another panic attack coming on.

In that moment, it was hard to fathom that here I was in a normal situation, having dinner at home after what I had gone through over the past month and a half, living through the pandemic and trying to overcome the assault.

My parents recognized that I was suddenly not OK and tried to console me. I was gasping for air as I tried to explain what was happening in my head and body. I remember thinking about the parks in Washington that I walked through on Capitol Hill since the beginning of the pandemic and seeing the armed soldiers day after day as masked residents walked by them.

"You don't understand what I just came from!" I managed to get out between gasps.

I felt as though I were in a movie that depicted the end of the world, but I was the only one who escaped. Only now, I was terrified to think about where I had come from. *I can't go back there.*

I knew that I was safe now, and I was in the right place. I became angry at what the government had forced us to live under in Washington and other cities that were locked down.

They had kept us locked down while North Carolina and other places like it were free. Forget about the attack that I had endured. I could not grasp the kind of society I had tolerated for the past six weeks.

CHAPTER 6

THE COVER-UP

I stayed with my parents beginning in late April and through much of the summer. The panic attack on my first night home turned out to be a preview of what was to come. I actually declined. I would wake up before dawn having a panic attack. I knew Dad would be up and getting ready by 6 A.M., so I would go into the living room and ask him to pray over me or talk with me to distract me from my thoughts and physical symptoms. I drank cups of calming herbal tea. I would double up on tea satchels and combine various teas, hoping they would help calm me down.

But I could not shake the anxiety. Intrusive thoughts kept popping into my head almost constantly. I would be shaking in bed throughout the night and finally drift off to sleep, only to wake up in a panic. I didn't know what was causing it. I had lived through the traumatic event at the beginning of April and the loneliness at the beginning of the pandemic, but I was not in immediate danger now. Yet in my mind, I thought I was.

As silly as it sounds now, I was still afraid of taking the benzodiazepine. I would take it every few days and it would help some, but I was still struggling.

I lost forty pounds in two months from not being able to eat due to the intense anxiety. I was usually able to get food down around dinner time, and that was what fueled me throughout this period.

I did not know what a nervous breakdown was, but I imagined that I was experiencing one. I felt like a dead person in a living body. I wanted to die and felt that I was already halfway there.

But I was also scared to give up and die. The idea of not existing anymore was so tempting. But realizing that death sounded good made me even more scared. I kept on going because I did not know any other choice. I was out of work again for a period in May, and then I went back because I had nothing else to do. It was a Catch-22 where the stories in the news scared me, but I needed work as a reason to get up every day. Reading a simple headline about the pandemic could send me into a panicked spiral.

I hope those around me will begin to understand what was happening in my head. I had to face it all again in writing this, but it reminds me of how sick I was mentally and how fully I have been restored since then.

All the while, troubles in the world were not improving. It seemed that civil unrest was actually getting worse. I had been at my parents' place for about a month, which was three weeks longer than I planned. I was also still paying $2,200 per month for my apartment back in Washington.

While in North Carolina with my parents, I watched from afar as the George Floyd riots played out—first in Minneapolis and then as they spread to Washington. I decided I was not going back as long as the riots continued. I worried that my apartment building, which had businesses on the first floor, would be attacked by looters. I was in no shape to sleep while lying in bed scared of the violence unfolding downtown.

Governors activated 17,000 national guardsmen in twenty-three states and sent them in to help. The Border Patrol assigned 350 of its agents to the frontlines in Washington, which I had never seen before. So much was happening at once.

In Portland, Oregon, rioters fought federal police day after day, week after week, and eventually month after month, attempting to take over and burn down a federal courthouse downtown. It was the first time many Americans heard of Antifa.

The violence in Washington as well as in Portland, where I had been downtown many times in high school, became personal to me. I knew those buildings. Rioters attacked police with explosives and machetes. Some people vandalized buildings to the point that the first floor exteriors were nearly unrecognizable.

More than 140 Department of Homeland Security and other federal police officers were injured defending the courthouse in Portland. Some of them were Border Patrol's tactical agents who I knew from my work on the southern border. It felt personal. These weren't just any police—they were people I knew who had been sent to defend a federal building in Portland without help from local and state authorities.

George Floyd had become a household name, but for me, it was a complicated acquaintance. Due to the timing of my attack in April 2020 and Floyd's death in May 2020 and all of my intensive therapy, my mind saved an image of Floyd's face as that of the man who attacked me. I still do not understand it.

Every time I saw Floyd's face on TV or in an online story, I would get nervous. It felt as though I had just seen the face of the man who hurt me on the street. I would consciously tell myself, "That is not the man who hurt me," and know that it was true, but his picture made me tense.

To this day, I do not remember the face of my assailant. I still see Floyd's face when I think of the attack, even though I know he had nothing to do with it.

Despite wrapping up EMDR treatment by the time I finally returned to Washington in late July, I still struggled when I saw a large Black man in sweats on the street, especially since my attacker was still at large.

I would cross the street to get away from him. My ability to be outside was much better than it was right after the attack, but I was still living in a way that I would not have before it happened.

Back in North Carolina, my parents tried to distract me from my anxiety when we weren't working. Because the state's pandemic protocols were so lax, we would go to local shopping centers and hang out there or watch movies or work on puzzles at home.

While living with my parents, they kept the mood light. They knew the news could upset me, so they tried to keep conversations and TV fun. Dad loved and still loves to go out to Starbucks for coffee.

My parents and I would walk around an outdoor shopping center in town and look in store windows, buy treats and hang out in Barnes and Noble, and walk around the many parks in the area. We would go out to dinner at Cava or another fast casual restaurant. We would walk around the Harris Teeter grocery store and debate whether the subs or the pizza were the better meal for that night. I went to church with them on Sundays when I was able to get out of bed. They really did their best to keep me in good spirits while also understanding that they did not fully grasp what was going on in my head. They were always willing to listen when I wanted to talk.

I did not believe that my mind could heal and stabilize until the world around me became a more quiet and peaceful place—and my assailant was off the streets and the court proceedings were done.

All the while, everything around me continued to get worse. The 2020 election was a few months away. The rhetoric around the presidential election was amping up, as well as the idea of our democracy coming under attack. These were normal talking points (maybe not *totally* normal), but in my state of mind at the time, they seemed to be reasons to panic.

One morning, I was in a particularly bad spot mentally. My father asked me to follow him outside. After I did so, he said to look up at the sky and my surroundings. I looked up at the sky then around at the many trees, the parking lot of neighbors' cars, the apartment buildings, and a dog being walked by its owner. He asked what was out of place or wrong or showed danger. I said that I did not recognize anything that fit those descriptions.

"Anna," Dad said, "if you didn't watch the news or read the headlines, you would have no idea that we are in a pandemic. You would have no idea about the looting, the riots, the protests, or the conspiracies about the pandemic. You would just know that it's a beautiful day and everything is fine. So when you get scared, just look outside and remember that if you did not know any different, everything would seem fine—because it is fine."

That anecdote has stuck with me. Every once in a while, I'll tell myself that line when the news gets to be too much, when mass shootings seem to be happening left and right, when a member of either political party makes a terrifying claim, or when things feel overwhelming. It always brings me back to my reality.

Police contacted me in early summer to say that they found a match to the DNA taken from the clothes I wore the day of the attack. They named the man who they believed had attacked me. He was homeless and lived very close to my apartment building.

That was great news. We had a name. He would not get away in the long-term. There would officially be a prosecution. The police would now work to arrest him.

While at my parents' home, my editor Keith assigned me a story on whether crime in Washington was up or down in the first few months of the pandemic.

I thought it would be an easy assignment. As a homeland security reporter, I worked with federal, state, and local law enforcement daily. I knew how to find police statistics. I had looked up crime stats for Washington in mid-2019 as I was looking to move from upper Georgetown to a more central part of town.

I had pulled up Washington's Metropolitan Police Department website and read about different types of crime—homicide, sex abuse, assault with a dangerous weapon, robbery, burglary, motor vehicle theft, theft from auto, arson, and other types of offenses.

In 2019, the map showed block-by-block details of the crimes, total and by category, that had been tracked around Capitol Hill and the H Street neighborhood where I was looking at apartments. I toured apartment buildings in that area and used the crime data to choose one that was reportedly safer than others. I selected Station House Apartments on 2nd Street NE.

I opened the Metropolitan Police Department's crime map to see the data on crimes reported since March. It showed that crime was, in fact, down significantly. I began to work on my story comparing pre-COVID trends with more recent data. I was impressed that the data from such recent arrests was already on the map.

While working on the story about crime levels in Washington, I decided to look up my case on the map. Back then, the D.C. police map showed pins where crimes actually took place. They now color code certain blocks or neighborhoods so it is more ambiguous.

I fed my details into the D.C. police crime stats filters: April 2020, sex abuse, with or without a weapon. My brow furrowed as the results popped up on the screen. No pin was placed at the location where I had been attacked. I wondered if they forget to include my crime on the map.

I looked at the map on the other side of the street: Station House, where I lived. No pin there either. Perhaps they had put a pin at the address on my driver's license. I checked, but there was no pin. What about my previous address? Again, no. No pin at my office or anywhere else as I frantically clicked on other dropped pins and read their descriptions. None were for the crime committed against me.

In Washington, it is possible to have four of almost the same address because the city is divided into quadrants, so there could be a 100 K St NE, 100 K St NW, 100 K St SE, and 100 K St SW. Perhaps the police input the wrong quadrant, so I looked up all the equivalent locations but came back empty.

I sat back in my chair, confused. My first and only thought that day was that the police were behind schedule and had not gotten around to posting my crime on the map. I was disappointed, but figured government bureaucracy was the holdup in updating the city crime map.

I emailed MPD. I explained that I was a national reporter and also a sex abuse victim and shared the details of my incident. I also mentioned that the U.S. Attorney's Office planned to prosecute the case.

I did not get a response that day or for days afterward, which was unusual given that in all other professional contacts with MPD, I heard back within a day or two at most.

A week went by, but I still had not heard from the police, so I followed up.

It was not until two weeks after my initial inquiry that MPD wrote back. The official stated in an email that my incident had not been forgotten. It had been purposely excluded from the crime stats. It was not a mistake. He explained that only first-degree offenses were included on the crime map.

I had not considered that they would have chosen not to include it.

I jumped out of my chair and walked over to the closet where I kept a binder of documents that the police and U.S. Attorney's Office had mailed me since April. I had to see what degree of sex abuse my attacker had been charged with.

Sex abuse in the third degree.

Did this attack not matter? I had never heard that all arrests and charges were not included on a police crime map. My case was not insignificant—the U.S. Attorney's Office was bringing charges on my behalf!

It also occurred to me that if the D.C. police were not including all crimes on the map, then my belief that I was picking the safest city block when I moved a year earlier was baseless. It was not amenities or floorplans that landed me at my new apartment building. It was the same crime stats page that I was now learning was based in half-truths.

The police officer had stated that even second-degree sex abuse victims were not counted. But there would be far more lesser-degree victims than first degree. To not include all degrees of sex abuse on the map was to ignore a huge bloc of people. And to treat those victims as if what happened to them was not significant enough to place a dot on a map invalidated their suffering. It communicated that the misery they had been through—not just in the crime they suffered, but also the aftermath—was not important and not worthy of mention, even though the Department of Justice prosecuted and the D.C. police department responded.

By not including me and countless other sex abuse victims in the crime stats, they took away our voice. Victims seldom speak out for many reasons—people will not believe them, they want proof, they do not care, or they are simply distracted.

That crime stats page is often the only voice for victims. It speaks for us and says, "Something happened to someone where this pin was dropped—and it matters."

The police decided we don't count. The D.C. police might as well have emailed me back saying, "Anna, it wasn't that bad. It's not a big deal. Calm down. You're fine. At least you weren't raped."

Where did they think the sexual assault against me was headed when the attack was interrupted and I was rescued? Was I supposed to apologize that I was saved that day and spared from worse? The police department in the nation's capital had invalidated the crime against me—a resident and a victim—even though it was their job to help. If a sexual assault did not count a few blocks from the U.S. Capitol, then where in America should it count?

My takeaway was that Washington's police and elected local leaders who came up with the idea not to count all felonies simply did not care about the impact of not including the stats on all victims.

Was I the only one who knew this? Had I just uncovered something significant? The system was rigged against regular people like me, and no one was talking about it. I was embarrassed not to have known about this, given my work with law enforcement. Why was no one talking about this? Had other victims of crime in D.C. realized this?

Coming to this realization that the stats were rigged by leaving out dozens, hundreds, maybe even thousands of sex abuses incidents in D.C. every year—not to mention other types of felonies—felt like a stab in the back. I vowed to expose it one day, but I also wanted this chapter of my life to be over. Who would care that my attack and others were not in the police stats? For now, it was just another grievance that I had to accept and find a way to live with.

The system was not meant to help me but to silence me. If the police had a choice, I wondered if they would even want my case prosecuted or would consider it meaningless since it was not a first-degree assault.

Victims are not numbers. We are people, just like every officer, every prosecutor, and every judge.

As far as why the crime stats were covered up, I tried to rationalize it and come up with a positive reason for it. I could not think of anything. I could only assume one thing: crime in D.C. was and continues to be covered up to make the city look safer than it is. It was a tourist Mecca. High crime levels downtown were not good for the city or the administration. It projected the appearance that even the president could not control his own backyard.

Covering up crime shows a lack of integrity on the part of the D.C. police. Why were the upper echelon of D.C. government and the MPD choosing not to count all crimes in the stats? Was it really to make D.C. appear safer than it was?

CHAPTER 7

THE RETURN TO WASHINGTON

It was July 2020. I was several months into therapy. After begrudgingly deciding to make the benzodiazepine a daily part of my recovery regimen, I started to feel better by July and August. I was still experiencing panic attacks, and my mind was certainly not back to normal, but I was making progress. I was finally able to look back at the previous few months and see that I had been mentally sick and emotionally devastated. When I was at my lowest point, I knew I was not OK, but I did not realize how bad I was.

I took the benzodiazepine every morning and occasionally later in the day. I was eventually able to reduce it to a few mornings a week, then two days a week, and then as needed. Finally, I was no longer using it except for the occasional panic attack, maybe once a week by the end of the year.

I had to learn to trust that the doctor prescribed the medicine to help me, not to harm me, but I also had to use it appropriately. Had I not been so concerned about its addictive properties, I would have taken it multiple times a day and probably would be in a different place now. Frankly, I would have gobbled it up.

I was still in North Carolina with my parents, but I was beginning to get updates about my case back in Washington.

My court case was moving slowly. I had been informed in June 2020 that the suspect had been identified through the DNA found on my clothes, which was a huge step forward. That he matched a profile already in the database was another enormous break. He had a criminal record, and his DNA was in the system because of that. Our case could move forward because there was someone to prosecute.

I was not surprised that the suspect had a criminal record. He seemed reckless.

The good news did not last long. Upon learning that he had been identified, authorities said he would be arrested. Police believed they knew where to find him since he lived on the street near Union Station.

Sure enough, I soon received a phone call informing me that he had been arrested. I was elated. At that very moment, I was safe. When I got back to Washington, I could walk outside and not have to worry about running into him on the street and having him recognize me. I had not known this feeling of freedom and safety in months.

That feeling passed within seconds. After being told the good news, I was warned that he had been released from jail the day after he was arrested.

I was told that because of the pandemic, the judge did not want to hold the suspect in the D.C. jail due to the close quarters. I felt that this man who I fought as though he were trying to kill me had more rights than I did. The criminal justice system was doing more to protect this dangerous man than to protect the public.

I received countless letters from the U.S. Attorney's Office and the Metropolitan Police Department in the two years after the attack as my case navigated through the legal system. I also received emails from the U.S. Attorney's Office, updating me on my case. Sometimes they would call, but more often, I received unsealed letters through the mail. My name, the suspect's name, the charges filed, and the case number were easily accessible to anyone who came across those letters. Every envelope had a Department of Justice label, which could have provoked anyone's curiosity.

Why make such a fuss over keeping my identity private as a sex abuse victim and then mail out more than a dozen unsealed letters? Many of those letters went from Washington all the way to Texas after I moved in 2021, and they managed to show up intact, even though they were open.

The U.S. Attorney's Office assigned a victim advocate representative to support me through the process. I was confused about her role for twenty-one months after she was assigned to me. It seemed to be a waste of an employee. I imagine she would have provided me with great support, but when I asked pointedly what she was supposed to do for me, I got a flimsy answer, so I unfortunately did not reach out to her during my two-year legal limbo.

As I navigated the process early on, I learned that I was eligible for compensation to cover some of my costs incurred as a result of the crime. I was eligible to claim up to $2,500 of therapy and counseling related to the attack. That was a big help, because my therapist was out of network with my insurance provider. She also charged $200 per session, and I was seeing her twice a week at the beginning. I ended up paying well above $2,500. I half expected that I would submit my therapy sessions for reimbursement and be denied by the city, but sure enough, they sent me a check. I was grateful for that policy. Someone in the D.C. City Council chose to advance that idea and make a whole pot of money available to victims of violent crime. And given that the crime stats do not actually show how many victims exist in Washington, I could only imagine how much money the city was spending on therapy for victims.

My case was filed in court on July 7, 2020, according to a piece of mail I received from the U.S. Attorney's Office. Normally a crime like this would be prosecuted by the district attorney in a city or county, but because Washington is not a state, felonies are prosecuted by the U.S. Attorney's Office. In simple terms, rather than having a regular county prosecutor take my case, the feds were prosecuting it.

It was incredibly validating, but at the same time it was confusing since the police didn't even acknowledge what had happened to me. It also seemed odd that they were taking this so seriously when they did not have the suspect in custody. If this was a big deal worthy of the feds, why did they allow him to be released? Why hadn't the U.S. Attorney's Office argued against it or done more to stop it?

What did it say about their concern that a sickness might spread among suspected violent criminals in jail rather than about the public being on the street with those same suspects?

I would correspond with my attorney via email but never in person because of the pandemic. Also, I would frequently receive letters in the mail that notified me of changes such as the defendant being charged. The case was supposed to begin in September 2020, but I was informed during the summer that it had been delayed until early 2021.

Then, in early 2021, my case was again delayed until late 2021. By that time, I had moved to Texas. I provided my new address to the U.S. Attorney's Office so they could continue communicating with me via mail.

I never met the U.S. attorney representative during the process. My attorney changed several months into the prosecution. I met my attorney in person for the first time nineteen months after the attack when I was in Washington to testify before the grand jury. Our first in-person meeting was also our only one.

I had never had a run-in with police or been a victim in a prosecution, so I had no idea how the system worked and what to expect. That was one of the hardest parts—wondering what was next and if these delays were normal. No one was telling me what was really happening behind the scenes.

What I do know is that every time I got a letter from the U.S. Attorney's Office, it prompted a great deal of conscious and unconscious anxiety. I sometimes received letters every few weeks.

I had signed up years earlier for a U.S. Postal Service program called Informed Delivery. The post office would email me a picture of the mail I was slated to receive each day. It was a great way to know if I needed to check my mailbox since I lived so far away from the mailroom in my new apartment building.

The downside was that every time a letter was to be delivered from the attorney, I would receive a notification in the morning. So before even getting out of bed, I would learn through my phone's email app that news was coming about my case. It spurred dread and anxiety that I would have to endure until I could get the mail late in the day. I would pull out the paper from the already-opened envelope and be reminded that I was not living a normal life. I was the plaintiff in a federal prosecution.

While I was trying to focus on healing, recovering, and moving on, a major operation was happening in Washington to bring my assailant to justice. It was hard for me to focus on anything but the prosecution.

I stayed with my parents for three months in North Carolina. I did not go back to Washington until I felt safe enough with the protesting and rioting that was still going on downtown. I insisted on returning to my old apartment, even though the suspect had been released from jail after his arrest earlier that summer. My mother took off work to drive with me back to Washington and stayed with me a few days as I settled back in to life there.

I was doing fine after my mother left—until I wasn't. Being stuck inside my old apartment, still unable to go back to work for nearly five months after the lockdowns had begun, was too much. I wanted to go out and live normally as I had in North Carolina. I was coming from a state where I could go to a shopping center and then out to eat as long as I wore a face mask, and even if I didn't wear one, it was not a huge deal.

I decided to move across town to Navy Yard into a new apartment building on the water. It would be a fresh start. At least I would see nature outside and would hear less city noise including people and sirens screaming on the street.

The city had a program to cover moving costs of crime victims, including the deposit on my new apartment.

But moving out was difficult. I felt that I was giving up and that I should try harder to overcome my fears about staying in my current apartment with the suspect at large. I was letting this man dictate my future and my life. I did not want to live in Navy Yard, but I chose that location primarily because he probably would never go there. I was making decisions based on my fear of him, not on what I really wanted. I did not want to move all the way back to northern Georgetown. No Metro station was nearby, and I needed that when the pandemic ended so I could go out again.

I told the property manager of Station House about my move. I was informed that I would have to pay $2,200 to break my lease. The money bothered me, but it was also about the principle. I was assaulted across the street outside my home.

This violent suspect was still on the loose and was not being held in jail. Even though I shared my reason for moving, Station House didn't seem to take me seriously. Right after the attack, I had alerted the leasing manager about the assault. I had thought she would send out an alert to residents. She didn't, so most residents were not aware of what had happened, that the violent criminal was on the loose, and that women should be especially careful outside the building.

Two years after the attack, I contacted the property management company. I spoke with someone in the leasing office and explained how I felt as a victim. This was the perfect example of how a corporate property management company seemed to put profit over people. The farthest I got was speaking to a leasing agent who apologized.

I moved out of Station House in September 2020. I hired a moving company and Ubered across town with my cat. The new apartment was even smaller than my previous one, but the distance from downtown was what I needed to try to start fresh.

I settled into my new apartment in Navy Yard. It was on the other side of the Capitol in a well-to-do area known in Washington as popular for Republican appointees and staffers to live in.

Days before the November 2020 election, unrest broke out in major cities, including Los Angeles, Portland, Washington, and Raleigh.

Hundreds gathered in the Black Lives Matter Plaza, a three-block strip running north of the White House. Hundreds of people, most dressed in black clothing and many carrying black umbrellas despite no rain, marched to the plaza and then to other parts of downtown Washington.

Marchers in Washington walked down the street carrying signs that read, "Burn down the American plantation" while chanting, "If we don't get it, burn it down!" Others shot off fireworks in the streets, lit a trash can on fire, and burned an American flag.

I was in the midst of it. I lived a mile from the U.S. Capitol, and my reporting was focused on civil unrest. Seven months had passed since my attack, and while I felt better, I was worked up about the stress outside downtown.

The election came. Buildings downtown barricaded their entrances and blocked all first-floor windows with large pieces of wood. The city looked like a scene out of a movie. But the anticipated violence did not happen in Washington. We all breathed a sigh of relief as the election passed.

One way that I was dealing with so much stress was by pulling out my hair—a little here and there, sometimes more than a little. After years of doing this, it got particularly bad in 2020.

A few days before Christmas, I set up an appointment at a curly hair salon to talk about how to cover up the bald spot on top of my head. It was odd to be able to go out for a hair appointment but not to go to work amid the pandemic.

"We have to shave it all off," the stylist said.

There was no "might want to," "possibly," "should," or "could" in that sentence. Just "we have to."

The night before the appointment, I took a shower. I knew it was possible that my hair might need to be cut off because I could no longer cover up what I had done. I held my hair in the shower, feeling the water and shampoo run through the strands. I clung to it. It had been with me through so much my entire life, especially over the past year, even as I had pulled it out. How would I know myself if I cut it all off? What would other people think? Would men lose interest in me? I wasn't trying to date, but I feared for the future. Would it take five years to grow back? Would I be able to stop pulling my hair out in the future? What if I had to keep it short for years because I couldn't stop pulling it?

Many women dye their hair when they are looking to make a big change in life.

Here I was, under so much duress over the past seven months that I had lost control of my hands and damaged my hair so much that it had to be shaved off for yet another fresh start.

While trivial in the grand scheme of things, the loss of my hair felt like I was losing an important part of myself.

After the appointment, I walked down 15th Street NW south toward the White House. I kept touching my head in disbelief, yet I accepted what I'd done. I felt liberated from hiding my hair-pulling for so long. My mom called it my Halle Berry look, and that inspired a lot of confidence in me.

Seven months into therapy, Susanne asked me to list my dreams—what I hoped for and what I wished would come true. I told her that I had completed all of them. I had moved back to Washington after college, landed another internship, worked my way up into a full-time job and then into media full-time as a breaking news reporter, and finally became a beat reporter covering a certain topic. I was unsure if I wanted to graduate from the *Washington Examiner* to a bigger news outlet. Many outlets had lost their appeal to me. Perhaps it was better to stay put rather than take on a new challenge.

My therapist brought me back to reality: "Anna, what are your dreams now?"

"I don't think I have any," I replied.

Susanne seemed surprised to hear that response. She gave me homework for the week: think of a dream or goal for my future.

I tried to complete that assignment over the next few days before seeing her again. I couldn't come up with a single dream. The only thing that filled my mind was how much I hated my present circumstance. I felt that I didn't have the mental capacity to dream. I literally could not dream if I tried!

I didn't have any career goals. I felt lost as I was bound to work at home indefinitely. I felt unlovable as a sexual assault victim as I struggled to stop myself from pulling my hair out.

I wanted to dream about the day that my federal case would be behind me. I imagined the relief in my head and body, knowing that it was over. But I couldn't imagine what my life would be like before then.

What I did not realize was that I was incapable of dreaming at that point. I was in a survival state.

What would or could I possibly dream for?

I spent Christmas at my grandma's home in Florida with my parents and sister.

My mother suggested that I wear earrings, which was her way of encouraging me to look more feminine with my haircut. I felt safe in keeping my hair short. Maybe if men thought I looked masculine, they wouldn't attack me on the street or proposition me at work. To be honest, I found great comfort in the haircut; it was almost like a protective mechanism.

I was also liberated from what society expected me to be. The short hair was a lot easier to keep up. The haircut was also demoralizing because it demonstrated that I did not have the strength to stop the hair pulling, and I had had to resort to serious action to address it.

I was getting into a pattern with work. The lobby in my new apartment building had a number of spaces where residents could work, but few used them, likely out of fear over the pandemic. They were typically empty. If someone was working there, others would be careful to remain at least six feet apart and wipe all surfaces down. I would spend mornings working downstairs in the lobby with my face mask on and then go back upstairs to my apartment for lunch. I would then return downstairs to continue working in the afternoons. I would even work sometimes until 9 or 10 P.M. because I was so bored with nothing else to do. An abundance of news was coming out of Washington, not far from where I sat on my couch. Working in public made me feel that someone was with me. I couldn't bear to sit alone in my apartment all day and night. I still hated being alone with my thoughts. I was feeling that recovering from the assault would never happen.

My case was supposed to go to court in the early fall of 2020, but I was informed that it had been delayed again until early the following year. Little did I know that January 6, 2021, was coming, and although a different part of the U.S. Attorney's Office prosecuted sex cases than the attorneys who would handle the January incident, my case would be delayed after that day.

It seemed that justice would never come. Here I was hiding in my apartment except to walk three blocks to the grocery store and to a rare doctor's appointment. And a man who had taken so much from me was somewhere out there, free—for now.

CHAPTER 8

THE FINAL STRAW

January 6th started out like any other day, but as the certification of the election results was underway, the unprecedented happened. I had had a medical appointment that day. I was coming home afterward in an Uber and walking into my apartment building when my phone started to buzz with notifications about people storming the Capitol. I went to the roof of my building to see the Capitol dome, which was not even a mile away. I could not see the action on the ground from the rooftop. I began writing a story about the situation as it unfolded. Coworkers were hiding in secure rooms in the Capitol. Everyone was taking cover on Capitol Hill. It seemed surreal. Was there a real threat? I couldn't find video coverage to see what was happening. I worked in my winter coat from the rooftop in case I could hear anything in the distance.

Protesters participating in a "Stop the Steal" rally in support of President Donald Trump breached a police security perimeter and stormed the Capitol, forcing lawmakers to abandon the House floor.

Thousands of people who marched from the White House down Pennsylvania Avenue NW to Capitol Hill descended on the west side of the Capitol Wednesday afternoon. Police moved to evacuate surrounding office buildings, including the Cannon and Madison office buildings, and the Library of Congress.

At about 1:30 P.M., police told the *Washington Examiner* that no one was allowed to leave the Capitol. Protesters rushed barricades on the east and west sides of the building; hundreds climbed up the building's front steps after pushing back the U.S. Capitol Police.

Minutes later, more than 500 House and Senate lawmakers were moved out of their chambers after protesters seeped into the building, somehow getting past metal detectors and security checkpoints, according to CNN. Flash bangs were heard outside the Capitol as several dozen police officers in yellow jackets rushed up the steps on the east side of the building.

I was concerned for my safety a mile away on the rooftop of my apartment building. I was also anxious about what the protesters might do to our city, but my biggest concern was for the countless people I knew on the Capitol grounds.

Things settled down by the end of the day as the National Guard was sent in. The events of that day would become an issue for debate by both Democrats and Republicans.

I woke up the following day in disbelief over what had happened.

A few days later, I walked to the Capitol with my press credentials to peek inside ahead of the Inauguration. What I found took me aback. Glass was cracked and broken in various places where violent protesters had tried to—and did—breach the building and get by Capitol Police officers. It felt eerie to stand inside and look through the broken windows on the east side and see soldiers and Humvees outside. This was not my Washington.

I was not in a place to make sense of what had happened on January 6th. I was distraught by what my city had become with the unprecedented level of security downtown. It was too much for me after going through a hellish nine months.

Ten days after January 6th, I went on a walk in the evening around the Navy Yard waterfront. It was a cold winter, particularly on the water. I rarely saw people out and about. I was feeling increasingly unsettled in Washington.

My court date had just been delayed again until later that year. My case had not even started, and it continued to be delayed. It would not begin in early 2021 as expected. I was walking over one of the footbridges that run along the water between the Major League Baseball team's park and the Navy Yard waterfront when I looked up at the night sky. I felt the cold pinch of the winter air on my cheeks. The river sat calmly next to me.

"I'm ready to leave D.C.," I thought. "I'm *going* to leave D.C."

It was not a debate or consideration any longer. I was at peace. I had made my decision without *trying* to make it. My mind told me that it was time to go, and I was OK with that.

For years, I believed that the only people who mattered in the world were those in Washington. I know that's not a very considerate thought.

Many of my old friends had come to Washington for a year or two, or maybe even a few years, and then left. When people left Washington, they were written off. They were not part of the club any more. A lot of people in Washington look at it that way.

So when I decided to leave Washington, I was saying that I did not care about what the city and its residents thought of me. I did not care if I stopped mattering to people here.

Maybe I was gaining clarity into what really mattered in life.

I was also realizing that the rat race, the lockdowns, the endless working from home, and the hometown turned into a lowkey war zone were not worth my sanity. I could not stay in a place just so I could continue to be relevant and matter. My pride died in a big way that day as I received a humility check that I needed. That humility check would be brutal and last for several years as I struggled to find my place in the world outside Washington.

The stories that I wrote in the days following January 6th were punishing on my mental health. I wrote about previous Democratic and Republican presidents condemning the attack and how the nomination of the Department of Homeland Security secretary, Chad Wolf, was pulled for not doing more to stop it. I also looked at the chain of command failures and what went wrong within security protocols during the Capitol's seizure and why it was not prevented or stopped sooner. I had as many questions as readers did. I worked hard to get answers, but some of those answers were simply not clear.

Some rioters were stuck in the city because they had been placed on the no-fly list and could not get out. Meanwhile, senators launched bipartisan hearings to investigate the attack. This meant we were going to be talking about it more in the coming weeks when Congress returned. One congressman, Jim Clyburn, suggested that rioters targeted specific offices in the Capitol that belonged to Democrats. At the same time, pipe bombs were found outside both the Democratic and Republican party headquarters.

It prompted new concerns for Inauguration Day on January 20th and what it could look like. Maxine Waters, a California congresswoman, said that outgoing President Donald Trump was trying to stir up a civil war. She said he must be stopped "dead in his tracks."

Questions remained about whether the Capitol attack was a coup, an insurrection, or domestic terrorism—or none of the above. Outgoing Trump administration officials, as well as Biden Cabinet members, confirmed that they were planning for nightmare Inauguration scenarios.

In an unprecedented move, the government and private sector partnered to lock down the downtown area ahead of the following week's Inauguration.

Normal security precautions for an inauguration entail blocking off streets in several locations a couple of days in advance. That year, neighborhoods near the White House, Capitol Hill, and in between the two famous buildings transitioned into fenced-in city blocks. Residents could not drive out of apartment building garages or even walk on the street without being questioned by police and having to provide identification that showed they lived inside the perimeter.

While the pandemic kept many at home instead of heading into the office for work, downtown streets were bare by Thursday, eerily silent. Some Washingtonians loaded up on groceries as if it were the onset of the coronavirus, but really it was in anticipation of the Inauguration.

Law enforcement personnel announced that they were aware of four plots to attack the Capitol ahead of President-elect Joe Biden's swearing-in ceremony.

Washington was swarming with law enforcement and soldiers. More than 20,000 National Guard personnel from the District of Columbia and neighboring states were in town to guard the Capitol and other federal buildings from mobs that could form in the days leading up to the Inauguration. Troops continued pouring in all week from as far away as Minnesota and Illinois.

The Metropolitan Police Department called in law enforcement from across the country to help. Up to 4,000 federal officers from the U.S. Marshal's Service were deputized and on the street.

The Department of Homeland Security moved its lockdown of Washington up by nearly a week at the request of Mayor Muriel Bowser, which allowed inaugural security forces to set up miles of barricades across town. Dump trucks, buses, and other large vehicles were parked in dozens of roads to prevent attacks from vehicles.

Acting DHS Secretary Pete Gaynor told department officials that the agency approved Bowser's request to begin security preparations on Wednesday, nearly a week earlier than planned.

The National Mall, where the public normally gathers to watch the swearing-in of a new president, was off limits to locals and visitors. The National Mall includes the Washington

Monument and stretches nearly a mile and a half east to the back of the Capitol, where the Inauguration takes place.

In addition, Biden and Bowser asked the public not to travel to Washington to attend Inauguration festivities.

A seven-foot-tall unscalable fence was installed around the Capitol the day after it was attacked. It was then expanded to various areas around the city. The same Capitol fencing was seen on 13th Street, despite White House plans to extend it only to 14th Street. Eighteen-wheeler trucks parked on K Street offloaded shipments of plywood near the White House Wednesday night as workers secured windows and doors on office buildings and eateries.

Airbnb announced all reservations in Washington for the Inauguration week had been canceled, including those through its subsidiary, Hotel Tonight.

The Washington Metropolitan Area Transit Authority shut down more than a dozen train stations located underground inside a security perimeter that includes the White House, National Mall, and U.S. Capitol. Trains were able to pass through the stations, but they did not pick up riders at those locations from Friday through Thursday.

"While we are supporting law enforcement plans to enhance security, we are also keeping essential services in place for our residents who need to get to work, to medical appointments, and to grocery stores," WMATA General Manager Paul Wiedefeld said in a statement.

Stations closing for seven days included Farragut North, Judiciary Square, Union Station, Archives, Arlington Cemetery, Farragut West, McPherson Square, Federal Center SW, Capitol South, Smithsonian, and Federal Triangle. Metro Center and Gallery Place closed a day later, starting on Saturday. Nobody could get in or out of downtown on a train, not that anyone was going anywhere amid the lockdowns, which were still in effect ten months after the pandemic began.

The Inauguration itself was uneventful, in a good way.

I would be getting out of Washington soon enough. I did not know where I was going or how soon, but I knew I was on my way out. For the first time in nine months, I had a glimmer of hope. I was not sad at the idea of leaving Washington, a place that was my home and that I also saw as my future. I needed a setting that would help me get out of survival mode.

Over the winter months, I plotted. I set my sights on somewhere free and warm.

My company agreed to let me move to Miami for six months, given my unusual circumstances. Our office was still not open due to the pandemic. No one on staff would notice that I was reporting from afar.

The Miami realty market was extremely competitive, even for a one-bedroom apartment on South Beach, so I enlisted the help of a real estate agent. As soon as a place would come on the market, it could be gone within hours, if not less than an hour. I was picky. I wanted the perfect spot, because after the year I'd had, I felt finding the perfect apartment would bring a turnaround in my life. The idea that bad things happen to me would flee if I could just find a good enough place to live and recover.

Often I was the most qualified applicant, but I would lose because others were offering to rent for twelve months and I was requesting only six months.

In March 2021, I packed up my apartment in Washington, the one that I had moved into only six months earlier. I sold furniture and put everything else I owned in a storage unit with the help of a moving company.

Then I said goodbye to Washington. I rented a car, packed up the cat, and drove south to my parents in North Carolina. We would stay with them for a week and then fly to Miami to continue the apartment search. I would take a breather on the beach and then hoped to return to a calmer Washington, where my federal case was still on the docket.

By June 2021, I had been living with my parents for two months. I had lost three apartments that I had made offers on, and the outlook was bleak. I had traveled to stay with my parents for what I thought was a week, but now it was heading into month three.

What started as a $1,500 search was now approaching $2,000 a month, for the same small one-bedroom apartments in South Beach that I began looking at in January.

I spent one morning in late June talking with my brother and sister. My brother was married with children in Austin, Texas; my sister was engaged and living in Nashville, Tennessee.

I felt caged in. I needed to make a decision soon, or I would keep on living with my parents.

I decided to change my plans and move to Austin. I had become an aunt a year and a half earlier, and I thought that being around children would be good for me. I had been to Texas many times for work, and it seemed more practical than Nashville if I were to continue covering the border. Also, I would be around family. It was a fresh start. I could find an apartment there, and when the time was right—after six months—I would return to Washington, which I hoped would be a better place with everyone going back to the office post-COVID.

My only regret about leaving Washington was that I had not done it sooner. Our office would not return in-person until the fall of 2022. As of early 2026, the company was still on a hybrid model with employees working from home two days a week.

CHAPTER 9

THE TEXAN TRANSPLANT

I was living in Austin. I started counseling with a therapist in town to process the move and to continue to address everything that I had lived through over the previous year. I did not realize at the time that even though the sexual assault had happened more than a year before, I was now coming out of more than half a year of solo living during the pandemic and the frightening events of the 2024 election, January 6th, and the Inauguration. I was out of Washington, but I was still on edge.

On July 15th, I flew to Austin from North Carolina with my cat. My brother, his wife, and kids were out of state on vacation for several weeks. They had left their minivan at the airport and mailed me a key to the van ahead of time, so when I arrived in Austin, I walked my two suitcases and cat carrier out to the economy lot, found the van, and got in.

The car was extremely hot. I was reminded that this was my new reality. I had just moved to Austin—this wasn't a vacation. It was my life. The heat didn't help. But it was in this moment that I wanted to be present. While I sat in the car with the doors open and engine running, waiting for the air conditioner to kick in, I didn't want to rush through and miss the fact that this was scary and new for me. It was my decision. After feeling powerless as a helpless victim in Washington with so much going on over the past year, I was now making the calls in my life. It was unbearably hot, but I would get used to it.

My priority was for the car to cool down so the cat would be safe and comfortable. She was as nervous as I was about being in a new place.

I set the minivan radio to a station with a familiar song to help me feel at ease—"Heat Waves" by Glass Animals. I pulled up directions on my phone and set it on the dash so I could find my way to my new home in North Austin.

Within a week of arriving in Austin, I visited a church and was connected to a group of other twenty- and thirty-somethings who lived in North Austin. I showed up the following Tuesday night to meet everyone, looking like a deer in headlights. Those people quickly became a family to me. I shared that I had left Washington, my home, as a victim of a violent crime. I didn't expect them to understand the world I came from or what I'd been through. I was also afraid that if I overshared, I would scare them away.

I probably overshared anyway. I was desperate for a community.

It was wild to discover how lax Texas was with the pandemic. In Washington, most churches were not meeting in person, and face masks were required for those that were.

People in Texas complained about the pandemic and its impact on normal life. I could not believe it. I had come from what seemed to be an alternate universe. Here, I felt free. I didn't want to tell those around me that they didn't know the half of what it was like in locked-down places like Washington. I was still trying to make friends.

All the while, I was still working. After the attack, my first few work-related trips to the border occurred later in 2020 when I convinced myself that I was mentally and emotionally stable enough to travel. I required a lot of medications to keep me calm for those trips. I thought by forcing myself into normal work tasks, I could snap out of my highly anxious, depressed state. But it did not work that way.

It was early fall in 2021. I had moved to Austin weeks earlier and just come back from a trip to McAllen, Texas. There I saw and interacted with hundreds of migrants who had just been released from the border and were allowed to remain in the United States. Most of them were families with young children.

I decided after returning to Austin to drive about 100 miles north from Austin to downtown Waco to spend a day at Joanna and Chip Gaines' Magnolia and Silos property. It was my favorite thing about Texas. I had been to Magnolia before while visiting my brother in Austin. The Silos felt like a safe space. I was happy, satisfied, and content when visiting there.

I first discovered the Magnolia brand in 2016 when I started watching *Fixer Upper* on HGTV. I was just getting into home renovation and decorating when I discovered the show in its third season. Something about Joanna drew me in to the show. Her designs seemed to be extensions of the people who would live in the spaces. They were not meant to impress but to be practical and to evoke a sense of home to the homeowners.

As Joanna and her husband began publishing books, I bought and read them. In a way, she has mentored me through her books and by her example. She is not a trained interior designer, yet millions of people have connected with the how and why behind her designs. Surely I could learn to face my own fears and try new things, focusing on how she had done the same. Later on in my three years in Austin, I went to Silobration at Magnolia. It was a celebration in the fall, and Joanna was talking about her memoir, *The Stories We Tell.*

I was sitting on the turf below the Silos, hooked on every word. I had preordered her memoir, and it would arrive in a few days. Her message that night as she spoke about the memoir pushed me to tell my story. It was not that I had something huge to share. I had thought about writing a book for the sake of processing all that I had been through, but I felt like an imposter. I viewed myself as an ordinary person. But so did Joanna. Her words helped me recognize that I did not need a secret code to overcoming trauma or an epiphany on life to write a book. I was worthy of sharing my story because it was mine. If people wanted to read it, that was just a bonus.

Back to that August day in 2021, I was at Magnolia Table having breakfast, sitting in a high-top chair that faced the gift shop. I had ordered pancakes and eggs and bacon, knowing it would be a great meal—and it was delicious. But as I ate and was nearly finished, I felt heaviness and tightness on the left side of my chest. I tried to shake it off. I told myself that I was just stressed and was imagining the discomfort. But it also began to hurt. I called my best friend, Tara, while I walked outside to the parking lot and told her how I was feeling. She encouraged me to go to the hospital to get checked out.

The last thing I wanted to do was go to to the hospital; it would detract from my plans to relax on this trip. I decided to go to the hospital anyway, because I had never experienced anything like this before.

I looked up an emergency room center and drove north on I-95. It was a half mile from the Magnolia Silos. I was so close to where I wanted to be, but I would make this pit stop to be sure that I was OK. The best case would be they'd tell me I was fine and let me go. Worst case? I'd be in the best place if I were having a cardiac event.

As soon as I walked in to the front desk and said that I was having chest discomfort, they brought a wheelchair around, told me to take a seat, and pushed me to a private room. They hooked me up to an EKG and other machines. The upper number in my blood pressure was 187. I don't remember the lower number. I didn't realize that it was extremely high and I was in danger, but the doctors did. As soon as the number popped up, more staff came into the room performing tasks that I did not understand. They began giving me intravenous medication. They did a chest X-Ray and a CT scan. The tests all came back normal.

They asked what was going on in my life. I shared that I was somewhat of a nomad, working what could be a stressful job interacting with migrants at the border. I also told them I recently left Washington under unusual circumstances and was trying to adjust to life in Texas. I didn't realize that I was leading a stressful life until I described it out loud.

Anxiety and stress were to blame for my chest episode, they said, but I didn't feel stressed. When the symptoms started, I was in a place I loved, eating a wonderful meal, and relaxing after a few busy days on the border.

"Exactly," one of the nurses said. She explained that sometimes it takes the mind a few days or weeks or even months to process what it has seen.

I tried to reason that I had been to the border plenty of times before. Why would I only now be having a different reaction to what I'd seen?

I tried to push back, but they reasoned with me that what I was living through was not normal. I was experiencing stresses in my job and in my own suffering, that were taking a very real toll on me.

I felt broken. I couldn't even do my job without having a massive anxiety attack in public afterwards. I could not have a normal weekend after working on the border a few days earlier.

The hospital released me, and I decided to stay the night in Waco to relax rather than head back to Austin. But the next morning when I woke up, I was so anxious that I decided before 7 A.M. to head back home. It was a frustrating reminder that overcoming the attack in Washington could not be forced. I could not will it to happen by doing hard jobs or any activities I had done with relative ease in the past because they might hit me differently now. I was a different person. I had been through trauma that caused me to relate to others differently, whether I realized it or not.

The attack in Washington and the fallout from it was making me more empathetic to those suffering around me.

When I was on the border, I saw people coming across and being detained under one of the international bridges. That was normal, but what struck me was the horror and tragedy that those families, adults, and children had been through. I could only imagine what they had experienced. I thought my life was hard enough, but it paled in comparison to theirs. I felt that I was doing an injustice reporting on the border and not doing enough from the perspective of migrants.

I was overwhelmed with guilt about it This was in the days and weeks after being in the hospital as I began to process not just the border trip, but also what it happened in Waco. I needed to understand why my body and mind were telling me to slow down and pay attention. I was not in the same state of mind as I was before the attack. I would have to tread lightly going forward.

Who was this new version of me, and could I continue with the same job I'd been doing for four years? Nothing specific was bothering me about the trip, yet everything about it bothered me. And I was bothered by adjusting to a new place and wondering what my life would look like when my six months in Austin were up and I had to return to Washington.

What would I do if couldn't do this job anymore? I was faced with some of the same terrifying questions I'd wrestled with in the initial weeks and months after the attack. Did I have what it takes to keep doing this job? Would I ever get past what happened to me in Washington?

One day after therapy in Austin, I went to a nearby thrift store.

Grief is so complicated. You never know when it will pop out and take over. You hate this thing that hurt you, but then you miss it and can't believe it's over.

I was at the thrift store looking at home items when I spotted a Washington picture book on a shelf. I picked it up and began to look through it. I saw places I'd seen countless times: the Jefferson Memorial; Pennsylvania Avenue NW as viewed from the White House; the U.S. Capitol; the Reflecting Pool; the pavement that I pounded thousands of times. Those places belonged to me. Seeing the pictures reminded me that I was outside the bubble of where I was at home and where I mattered.

Without realizing it, I had tears running down my cheeks as I stood there flipping through the pages.

I remembered that excited feeling in my chest when I'd look down Pennsylvania Avenue toward the Capitol and instinctively knew my place in that world.

I missed standing in line at the U Street Trader Joe's with chiefs of staff, TV producers, think tank policy fellows, and politicians as we waited to purchase groceries.

I missed the Tidal Basin as it froze in winter and was perfectly silent at night.

I missed the happy hours on 14th Street after work.

I missed feeling like I was a part of something bigger than myself.

I missed the purpose I found in my work while being surrounded by those who also wanted to do great things.

There's no "how to get through grief" workbook to tell you that you're doing it right or wrong or how close you are to being through this hard part of life. That was the hardest. I'd break down crying randomly, such as that day at the thrift store.

Maybe the upside of the ebbs and flows is having a name for the process and realizing that I'm not lost in it. I'm grieving. And that's OK.

I was sad that I had to leave Washington even temporarily. I'm still confused about why I had to be the victim of the attack.

Part of my grief was the result of realizing that I over-valued meaningless things.

Without those things, I felt lost. I thought I had built my life on faith in Jesus, but I actually thought my purpose was found in my success and worth as a reporter. I was only as good as my most viral tweet or best TV clip.

Outside Washington, I had an opportunity to rebuild my foundation, which I wouldn't have realized was made of sand if I had not been yanked out of the capital city.

The grief was confusing, but it gave me the chance to evaluate the pain of what I had lost and rebuild my life on more meaningful things. I used this chance to stake my life and values on my faith in Jesus as my Savior.

There's a God who loved me too much to let me stay as I was. Maybe God was using the attack for His good in me after all.

"There used to be rules to crime," my friend Beverly said to me.

Beverly Hallberg and I were filming a podcast for the Independent Women's Forum in spring 2024. We were talking about my reporting on the border. I was also sharing a little about my attack in Washington when Beverly raised a bigger question: Is there a woman anywhere in the country who has not taken into consideration where she is going, at what time of day, on what route, how she is dressed, and how she responds to men around her?

Examples include choosing to go to stores while it's still light out, avoiding certain blocks or parts of town, taking Ubers or Lyfts instead of the bus or Metro, etc.

The idea was that women often avoid alleys at night because they're led to believe that criminals lurk in such places.

I did everything right on April 4, 2020. And yet this happened to me. And that was really a pivotal moment for me.

Beverly pointed out that we were both under the impression that as long as we took the right steps to avoid unsafe situations, we could escape crime. She also said that what was so senseless and upsetting was that I did everything right and made all the proper calculations, but I was still attacked.

The "rules" of avoiding crime—not going out at night, going out with someone else—had flown out the window after my attack.

Beverly hit the nail on the head.

I did everything right that day. I purposely waited to go to the post office until the weekend morning. I was not scantily dressed—although to be clear, no woman is asking to be assaulted or harassed because of how she is dressed. I wasn't approaching men on the street and creating problems.

In fact, I looked gross that day. I was wearing a baggy, worn-out black Nike hoodie and loose-fitting sweat pants. I had no makeup on except eyeliner. My hair was in a messy bun. If anything, men would see me and run away, not toward me.

If I could not run a weekend errand in a safe part of town while looking rough, then there was no way to safeguard myself on the street. It said to me that there are no rules. You can't do things "right" and expect to stay safe.

That was also why I left Washington.

I realized there was no way to stay safe. There was no logic.

It is comforting but also troubling to accept that I didn't do anything wrong that day, because it also means that I couldn't have changed anything to prevent it from happening again. Of course I wanted to know if I could have done anything differently.

But what about the near certainty that I did everything right and was attacked anyway?

How do we live when there are no rules for crime?

Because if I knew that I failed, I could do better next time.

CHAPTER 10

THE GRAND JURY

In November 2021, the U.S. Attorney's Office contacted me. I was informed that I would need to travel to Washington to testify before the grand jury since the case was finally moving forward. I had not returned to Washington in a year and a half since I fled.

I had asked my employer to allow me to remain in Austin where it was more convenient to cover the southern border, which faced the highest-ever number of monthly illegal immigrant apprehensions under President Joe Biden. My boss agreed that it was a good setup and told me to continue working from Texas. I was relieved. I was still thinking daily about where my life was going. Would I stay in Texas for another year or forever? Would I work remotely like this for years to come? What was next for me?

I don't say this lightly: I felt like a refugee in my own country when I left Washington and moved to Texas. I didn't want to be in Texas, but it seemed to be the next best option. It wasn't lost on me that I was reporting on refugees and immigrants who had been displaced after losing their homes. Here I was in my own country, like a refugee and nomad, wandering around and trying to figure out where to live, escaping the chaos back home where I didn't feel safe. Even though the trauma from the attack had unfolded in April 2020, I was still living in its aftermath. The attacker was still in Washington, living on the street near my old apartment.

The idea of returning to Washington terrified me. I asked the U.S. Attorney's Office if my mother could be present for the grand jury. I could not imagine facing it on my own. They agreed to cover the cost of my mother's flight, and we would share a hotel room.

On December 14, 2021, my mother flew from North Carolina and I flew from Texas to Reagan National Airport. We flew in around the same time and then took a rideshare to our hotel near Capitol Hill, roughly half a mile from where I had been attacked. This was the last place I would've chosen, but the attorney's office placed us there because of its proximity to the grand jury where I would testify the following day.

The next morning, my mother and I woke up early and decided to visit Union Station. I wanted to return to near the scene of the crime and take a moment to reflect and to convince myself that I was in a position of power now, even though I was scared that day. Later, I posted a picture on Instagram with a caption saying that I had returned to Washington to testify before the grand jury and to take back my power. It was meaningful to me. My mother took a picture of me standing with a hand on my hip in front of Union Station facing the Capitol.

We then walked several blocks to the U.S. Attorney's Office and entered the office of the victim advocate. It had a bold blue wall inside. We waited at the reception area, but no receptionist was behind the counter. We waited for about fifteen minutes before someone came out and introduced herself as the victim advocate. She took us upstairs to meet the attorney who would guide us through that day's proceedings.

The attorney took us into a large conference room. Both women expressed their condolences for what I had been through, and they were professional. I wondered how many other victims they helped in a year.

They shared with me that because I had traveled from out of state, I would not be able to appear in person before the grand jury, which was gathered in a room on another floor.

I almost laughed out loud. It was absurd to me that after my effort to be present in Washington that day, I could not appear in person before the grand jury. I was considered a health risk due to the ongoing pandemic. I could have testified over Zoom from Texas, I thought. Who had imposed such an absurd rule? Would a crime victim living in northern Virginia from across the Potomac River also be barred from appearing in a room before the grand jury? Technically, that person would also be from out of state, imposing a greater health risk on others. This was on par for Washington. These illogical rules were in the same class as the judge's orders to release the man from jail five more times after he attacked me. In my mind, without double standards, the criminal justice system would have no standards at all.

The women said I would be in a room with a camera that would record my testimony. It would be shown on a screen to the grand jury, which would be in the adjacent room.

Before heading into the grand jury room to be filmed, the attorney let me know that she would be playing a recording of my 9-1-1 call from the day I was attacked. She said she would play the recording for me beforehand so I would be prepared.

I told her to play it. She pulled up the recording on her computer and hit play. As it started and I heard my voice from that day, I suddenly let out a terrifying scream in front of my mother, the attorney, and the victim advocate.

I could not control my mouth or body. This troubling scream was different from the moment of the attack when I had screamed for help. I was having an involuntary reaction that I could not control. It felt as if all the pent-up fear from the previous twenty months came out in that moment. I was embarrassed, watching myself as if from a second-person perspective as I cried out.

I started sobbing hysterically and was gasping for air. But I wasn't making a conscious choice to cry. My body was involuntarily reacting.

Frankly, it scared me. After all of the therapy and time that had passed, how was I unaware of this frightened woman who was still in me?

That moment has stayed with me. I didn't know the trauma that was stored inside me until it was forced to come out.

The attorney led me to another floor, where I would speak on camera before the grand jury that was seated in the room next door. Despite just being in the same room with me, the attorney returned to the grand jury. She was to question me on camera, which again seemed ironic since I had just been around her. Now she was standing in front of the grand jury, potentially spreading any germs that I brought from Texas.

She asked me what I had been doing on the day of the attack. I said that I was on my way to the post office to mail an item I had sold on eBay. She asked what the attack entailed and what my attacker looked like. I told her the man who assaulted me was tall, large, and had dark skin. He appeared to be between thirty-five and fifty years old. The questioning lasted a little over twenty minutes. At the end, the attorney told me that I had done well.

I left the grand jury room relieved. It seemed to be a fail-proof case. It was a sexual assault that was stopped before it got any further.

My mother and I walked a few blocks from the attorney's office toward Chinatown. We ate lunch at an Israeli café. We were celebrating that the grand jury was finally behind me as we dipped into some of the finest hummus we ever tasted. We had our carry-on suitcases with us since we wouldn't be heading back to the hotel. We would be flying out in a matter of hours. I felt as though I would fall asleep at any moment and my body felt heavy.

We took a rideshare to the airport and checked in. On the ride to the airport, I had begun to shut down. I felt many emotions, but I also felt nothing. My mind was going in every direction, but it also felt empty.

I had just returned to Washington, which was quite a feat in itself. I had visited Union Station, the scene of the crime. I met with the U.S. attorney and victim advocate for the first and last time. I had testified before the grand jury. Now I was heading back to Texas. My mind could not process everything that was happening. It effectively decided to go into sleep mode as a signal that it could not handle any more.

I remember taking a picture with my mother before we went to our gates. I cried in her arms. I was relieved that this ordeal was behind me, but I also did not want her to leave me. I felt like a child, longing to be cared for and coddled.

In a post to Instagram that night, I wrote:

> I call my best friend "mom." Couldn't have had a better in-person support today. It was ugly at times. It was beautiful at others. It's over and that's the best part. I felt and knew I was covered in prayer. Every room I walk into didn't feel dark. They felt welcoming. I found my voice in a way that surprised even me. I roared and fought for myself. I didn't leave anything on the line. The next three weeks are out of my control but it's the time by which to accept our plea [deal]. If by Jan. 7, he has not, I will have to make a decision of whether to go to trial or drop the charge. The trial would not be until 2023 now because the subsequent misdemeanor charges he racked up while being out on bail after his arrest with me take priority for going through court before the more serious felony one. I am praying every day God moves his heart and brings him to take our plea so I don't have to decide what to do. But for now, my work is done and it feels so good. I'm so proud of what I did and who I have become and that I advocated for myself.

Now we would wait. Following the grand jury, the U.S. attorney offered the defendant a plea deal. He would have to decide whether to accept or reject it. The plea deal was a watered-down version of the maximum sentence that he could receive for a charge of sex abuse in the third degree. I don't remember the exact amount, but I think it was about nine months. At that point, he had been detained in jail for a month since our case was finally moving forward.

I hadn't wanted to extend a plea deal. I didn't think he deserved a shorter sentence for pleading guilty. Frankly, I wanted to throw the book at him. But the way the attorney explained it to me, it seemed that I would be foolish to question her recommendation, so I went along with it.

It was December 25th, Christmas night. I had spent the evening with my parents, my sister, and my brother and his family at his home in Austin. I was driving home to my apartment in North Austin, wrestling with all that was on my mind: the plea deal, the fear of going to trial, the pressure of having to decide, the overwhelming depression that had gotten worse recently, and the feeling of being lost in Austin even after five months. I was spending time with my family, but I didn't feel seen or known. I felt that no one understood my suffering, which made me feel alone and hopeless.

As I drove onto the 183 on-ramp, I thought, "I should give up. I don't want to live anymore." I had not had a thought like this since 2020, right after the attack. This one came out of nowhere, and it was genuine. I was so tired of moving forward. I just wanted to rest. I wanted peace. I thought dying was how I could achieve that.

I entered my apartment and sat on my couch. I wanted to die. I didn't know where this was coming from or why or what it meant. Should I die? I didn't really want to die. I was so confused. I called a friend for support. I didn't know why this had suddenly come over me.

The following morning, I woke up having a panic attack and decided to go back to my brother's house where my parents were still visiting. I did not know if I should tell them what I was thinking. I didn't want to scare them, but I was also scared for myself. I was still more afraid of dying and the permanence of it than the promise of rest by death. So I ratted on myself, hoping that they could set me straight.

They were confused. How had I gone from seeing them on Christmas night to suddenly saying that I wanted to die? I tried to play it down by saying that I needed support and hugs and wanted to be around them to help me feel better.

I had purchased a gun when I first moved to Texas as a way to defend myself. I'd talked about this with my therapist in Texas, and although she did not share her opinion, I could tell she did not think it was a good idea for me at that time. Looking back, I also don't think it was the best idea, even though I bought it for self-protection.

I also obtained my concealed carry permit in the state of Texas, which required going to a class for several hours and then passing a shooting exam.

As my mental health declined following the grand jury into January, I began to fear the gun. I saw it as a threat. Yes, I wanted to be dead. I hit a point of overwhelming exhaustion to the point that I just wanted to be done. I knew the gun would have been a way to do that. But I was also fearful of the gun itself. I was worried that in a moment of weakness, I might use it. I also feared the knives that I had in the house. It was a little irrational, but the more I thought about them, the more afraid I became. None of my knives were professional grade. In fact, they all had been purchased from such places as Marshall's and HomeGoods. I also still had the one the ICE agent had given me years earlier.

As I look back, I can see how overwhelmed I was with the grand jury appearance. Just being in Washington again was still registering with me. It had been a tense month, and that was not going let up any time soon. I figured the intense stress would dissipate once a decision was reached on the plea deal.

Naturally, nothing happened on time.

Two weeks after we were supposed to get a decision, we finally heard back. On January 20th, I received the news.

I had been at the Texas Public Policy Foundation's policy conference in Austin that morning when the attorney contacted me. I was covering the conference for work.

The attorney had written me to share that the defendant had accepted our plea deal.

I would not have to go to trial. We finally had the answer we had been waiting for.

In a post on Instagram, I shared a picture of me with my two oldest nephews and a rainbow sprinkle cake that I had bought to celebrate the defendant taking the plea deal:

> Yesterday, we celebrated. It felt weird to have some happiness and relief after 21 months of setbacks and disappointments. The defendant accepted a deal from the U.S. Attorney's Office to plead guilty for assaulting me in DC in April 2020. It means we won't have to go to trial—I am relieved. He will be sentenced to federal prison on March 25. As relieved as I am that he accepted our plea after three months of refusing it, it is uncomfortable to think something that happened to me was worth someone going to prison. Pray with me as I work through that. I bought a sprinkle cake because I'm believing my future is bright. Here's to celebrating how far each of us has come even when it can still feel hard. The worst is over and I've been delivered. Thank you, GOD.

CHAPTER 11

THE BORDER CRISIS

It took another three months to get through this bout of severe depression. My medical team played around with medications to help me, but as the sentencing day of March 25, 2022, got closer, I was increasingly on edge.

I continued to work and travel to the border in early 2022. I thought almost daily about quitting my job and working full-time in retail because it seemed easier on my mental health, but I was afraid to walk away from all that I had worked for. It wasn't that I actually hated the job; it was that I needed a lighter load in general. But I felt I couldn't leave it behind. What if I wanted back into the media after I left?

March 25th finally came. I don't remember if I took off work that day or just ducked out for a couple of hours to watch the sentencing on my computer. I did go over to my brother's house and sat in their second bedroom. I didn't want to watch this alone. I wanted to at least have people I knew and loved nearby for support.

I opened up the webcast and saw him. It was the first time I had seen the defendant in almost two years since he ambushed me on the sidewalk in April 2020. He was not facing the camera, but I didn't really want to see his face anyway because I didn't want to remember it.

I had a chance to read my victim impact statement. It could be as short or long as I wanted it to be. It was my chance to go before the judge, defendant, and everyone else and share how being a victim of this crime had impacted me.

I shared it all. And I told the judge how angry I was that this man had been released immediately from jail every time after his five arrests between April 2020 and November 2021, including for exposing himself to someone outside the Supreme Court, for violating the restraining order outside my apartment, and for being caught in public with a machete. He had been let out back onto the street every time. It didn't matter that I was getting justice in the end. It mattered that I had not received justice all along.

And I told the defendant that I forgave him. He said he was sorry for the pain he had caused.

I had expected it to feel liberating to share that with him, but it didn't. I had to forgive him knowing that he may not stop hurting people and may not "learn his lesson." That was difficult to accept.

In the midst of this, the attorney informed me of news that she had not been permitted to share with me until sentencing. The sentence he received today would be not only for my attack and the five arrests he sustained since, but also for attacking an off-duty female police officer in the same area of Washington prior to attacking me.

Another woman victim was watching the sentencing. She was getting the same justice that I was. All along, I had not been the first woman to be attacked—I was just one of them. It made the judge's decision to free this man repeatedly even more suspect and careless.

It was a morning of closure, but also of shock. Just when I thought my case would be wrapped up nicely and would be over, there was the unanticipated detail about another victim. I would never learn who she was, but I felt connected to her. We had both been assaulted by the same man and had survived. Here I was, with no police training, and I had escaped from his clutches. I felt incredibly fortunate and protected to have made it out alive. It became clear to me that this man had something against women. These attacks seemed targeted.

To this day, I don't know why he went after either one of us.

Here's what the judge in my case and others already know, but the public may not be familiar with: ten percent of perpetrators have five or more felony convictions, according to RAINN's analysis of crime statistics.

More than half of perpetrators will be released while awaiting trial. "For every 1,000 suspected rape perpetrators referred to prosecutors, 520 will be released—either because they posted bail or for other reasons—while awaiting trial," RAINN's website states.

We cannot accept this.

It goes further: only seven percent of perpetrators will be rearrested. It's what makes my case unprecedented. And this is what makes the court's handling of my case even more of an outrage.

I spent a month shy of three years in Texas. My time in Texas never felt natural or like home to me. Having grown up in the northeast and having spent the last seven years in D.C., I was homesick for the East Coast.

Even though moving out of Texas would mean leaving behind my brother, sister-in-law, and three nephews, it was evident that by the last six months of living there, I had become strong enough mentally and emotionally to consider returning to the East Coast.

In early 2024, I started to let myself dream. Where on the East Coast would I live? I knew the idea would have to be approved by the company, but it seemed to be the perfect time. The border crisis that had surfaced under President Joe Biden couldn't continue for more than a year if he were to lose the 2024 election. I was willing to bet that he would not win another term.

I wanted to put roots down somewhere. I was almost thirty-five years old. I still wanted to get married and possibly have kids, but I didn't know where I wanted to make that happen. To me, the longer I stayed in Texas, the longer I was delaying the fulfillment of my dreams.

So I began to list the features that mattered to me in a new place. I knew I wanted to be on the East Coast, but between Florida and Maine, I had no idea where to go. I wanted to be somewhere historic, within a half-hour drive of the ocean, with seasons but not too cold, and that was safe.

I had lived the city life in Washington. I did not think I wanted to return to living downtown in a city. My time there had been enough to scratch that big-city itch. Even in Austin, I had lived near downtown not far from the Whole Foods on North Lamar. I wanted to live somewhere close enough to what I needed, such as the post office and coffee shops, but where I could go to sleep at night and not hear noise. I was looking for a town that could be the setting of a Hallmark movie, where neighbors greet each other on the street and residents support local businesses. I actually searched online for towns on the East Coast where Hallmark movies had been filmed.

As I was considering all of this, one city came to mind. It checked all of my boxes, but I had never been there. So a Texas friend traveled with me to Georgia in 2024 to find out if I could see myself living there. It didn't take long to realize that this would be a great place for me. I wasn't looking for anything in particular; I was simply getting a feel for the town.

I decided to move forward with plans to move. I told my closest family and friends. In moving to Texas blindly, though I had family in town to lend me support, I had proven to myself that I could go somewhere and start over, even while in terrible shape mentally.

I knew what it took to make friends and how to meet people. I didn't need an army but just a few close friends who felt like family, and that would happen over time. I knew how to approach people and make them feel comfortable and to create a community that felt like home. I knew that I should not be sitting at home endlessly watching TV. I needed to get out and talk to people and to exercise regularly for my own good. And I knew I wanted to spend a lot of time outside. Texas was not only extremely hot, but also the terrain never appealed to me. Summers on the East Coast are hot, but the ocean and coastal landscapes really appealed to me.

I decided to move forward. I sold my 2009 Honda Civic, which I bought in Texas through Facebook the first month after I moved there. It was my first car. I had never owned one because in Washington I didn't need one.

I bought a newer used car that was much more dependable. I decided to sell all my furniture and take only what fit into my new midsize SUV. What I had in that car was all I would take to my next place. I wasn't hiring a moving company because everything could be replaced.

Another factor that pushed me over the edge to leave Texas was losing my ten-year-old cat, Saja, on February 15, 2024.

I had been in the process of deciding whether to leave Texas when Saja passed away unexpectedly in the early morning hours after Valentine's Day. I had adopted her as a rescue when she was a year old. We got to spend nine years together, and she was my only pet in that time. She was my sidekick, the girl I always came home to and took care of, and who loved me as much as I loved her. She was the only one aside from God who had been with me through all my struggles. She was there after the attack. She saw me cry and shake with anxiety, dance in my apartment, and sing to Lana Del Rey. She saw me learn how to meal prep. She watched me scroll on eBay for vintage Ann Taylor. She was just a cat, but she saw the unfiltered me.

She seemed to be perfectly healthy, until suddenly she was not. I was awakened early in the morning on February 15th by a loud scream in the living room. I jumped out of bed and grabbed my phone and turned the camera on. I wanted to start recording because I thought she was meowing loudly at the neighbor's cat that had recently started visiting her through the patio doors. I ran a short distance into the living room and unintentionally recorded Saja's final moments. She was lying on her side on the floor as she exhaled one long, final breath. I tried to resuscitate her, even though I didn't know how. She had let out a terrible scream and had taken her last breath, and then she was gone. She died in front of me as if to share her last moment with me.

Suddenly, I felt as if I were thrust back into the moment after the attack in 2020. I couldn't think. I didn't understand what had just happened. She was fine the night before. I had planned to go out on Valentine's Day, but my plans had fallen through, so I stayed in that night, made dinner, and spent the evening on the couch with Saja.

I had some of the same thoughts in the days and weeks after her death that I did after being attacked. I was trying to understand what led to this, what signs I missed, and how I should've handled her final moments. I beat myself up for not having handled it better.

I assumed I hadn't done enough to prevent this and that it was my fault. I should've seen the signs in her health, even though I still didn't know what they would have been. I should've had her on a better diet.

I thought I should've had more tests done as she was getting older to see if her health was declining in ways we could not see.

I couldn't imagine moving forward after all that I had been through without her by my side. But at the same time, she had gotten me through such a difficult season in my life as I was navigating Washington alone, leaving for Austin, and taking a couple of years to make sense of this new place. She had left me about a month and a half after I started to think about leaving Texas.

I thought back to 2020 when my therapist asked me to list a dream or a goal that I had, and I couldn't come up with anything. I knew no city could satisfy every part of me, but now I wanted to be somewhere that I loved and could continue to fall in love with.

I had thought that place would be Washington, but it wasn't. Now I had the rare opportunity to choose where the rest of my life would unfold, or at least the next couple of years. This would be my choice. I wasn't running away from Washington as I had before. I was now in a good place to dream and to have choices.

I lost what mattered to me most in my day-to-day life when Saja died. After all that I had endured over the previous few years, losing my cat was the final straw. My family had been expressing their concern for how I would handle her death one day, but no one expected it to be so soon. They scared me into believing that I would be an irreparable mess. But after what I had been through in 2020, it was as though I had a higher tolerance for pain. I grieved hard for the first month after Saja's passing until I had no more tears to cry.

In June 2024, with the car packed up so high that I could barely see out of the back window, and with Saja's ashes carefully buckled in the passenger seat, I set off for a new beginning.

CHAPTER 12

THE EAST COAST RETURN

Life back on the East Coast suited me well. In Texas, I had struggled to fit in. I wasn't into hiking, paddle boarding, river tubing, drinking at bars, two-step dancing, or attending music festivals—these were popular activities in and around Austin.

On the East Coast, I was in a new environment living in the Southeast within an hour of the beach, but I was back on the coast that was my home, not in the middle of the country. I had chosen a town that felt like the set of a Hallmark Channel movie. It was a safe place. I no longer trusted any police department's crime stats, so I didn't even attempt to check them when I made my decision to go to Georgia.

A few months into living in my new hometown, I was on the phone with my editor, Marisa, talking about the adjustment. "I really love it here," I said. "I've already got two hobbies, and I never had hobbies in Texas. I'm now into hunting and shooting."

There was a pause on the phone. I smiled because I knew she was confused.

"By hunting," I explained, "I mean hunting for seashells on the beach. And by shooting, I mean shooting photographs. I love the architecture down here."

I discovered a part of me in my new town that I had not realized was missing. I would engage in my new hobbies frequently, and I still do. They connected me to this new place and helped make it feel that I belonged there and that it could be my real home.

The five-year anniversary of April 4, 2020, came along. I had vowed a year earlier to write a book, and I was about one-third of the way into it. But I struggled to move forward because I did not know how to end my story. This couldn't just be a book of ranting and complaining. It had to have a solid ending, but what could that be? My life was good, and I was in the best shape mentally than I had been in five years, but I felt that something was missing.

I was happy even though my life had taken a drastic turn over the previous few years. I didn't feel lost and disconnected from Washington anymore as I had in Texas. I was involved in my new church, I saw friends weekly, and I enjoyed meaningful relationships. I was on top of my work, traveling as needed. I knew my neighbors in my apartment complex and hung out with them frequently. Everything felt good.

I told my closest friends that I planned to get on a dating app. They were excited for me. I didn't feel that I was missing anything in my day-to=day life, but if I were to met a man who grew from a friend into something more serious, I would welcome it.

I had also begun taking small steps to improve my physical health. After the 2020 attack, I initially lost weight due to the severe anxiety. As I started taking medication and began to feel better and then moved across town in Washington amid the lockdowns, I wanted to quell my stress and anxiety. While in Texas, I turned to food to comfort me as I had years earlier. My freezer was full of family-size pizzas, pints of ice cream, and other junk food. I had no fruits or vegetables. Everything was processed. The "food" was made of chemically engineered ingredients meant to drive the body to crave more. And that was what happened to me.

For several years after the attack, I ate. Food allowed me to stuff down feelings that I did not want to feel and thoughts that I did not want to face. A part of me still struggled to accept what had happened to me. I didn't know what the rest of my life, much less the next few years, would hold. Would I be single forever? What if I were ever a victim of crime again? Would I be able to handle that ordeal? What if I stayed in my new hometown for decades? Could I continue working remotely for my company? What did I want to do? Yes, I enjoyed shelling and photography, but was I just trying to avoid thinking about what mattered, or was I actually relaxing and having fun? Where was the line between the two? Was there something I wanted to do other than work as a reporter? What would I do if I knew I couldn't fail?

I had gained more than 60 pounds between late 2020 and late 2024. I put it on within months, and then my weight held for a few years as I would starve myself all day and then binge at night.

After moving to the East Coast, I found a virtual women's health company that seemed as though it could help me. Having eaten as I had for several years, I was obese, pre-diabetic, and very close to the threshold for diabetes. I was having trouble sleeping and walking due to hip and back pain. I hid from TV interviews and social media because of how I looked. I also suffered with a host of other medical issues that started in 2021.

But the biggest side effect was that I was disappointed, embarrassed, and ashamed of myself. I had eaten myself into obesity. I told my concerned family members for years after the attack that I was going to start taking care of myself. I just didn't know where to start, and I struggled to break free from the foods I craved.

My new doctor put me on an intense plan. Over the next few months, a few pounds began to come off. In April 2025, I pushed myself to take action on a health goal that I wanted to tackle for a long time: weight lifting. I wanted to learn the names of my muscle groups, what moves and machines and free weights could target them, how to lift, how to recover, and how to be consistent. I asked a neighbor who lifted weights if she would show me the ropes. Several weeks into doing the routine she set up for me, I started feeling more confident. Even the idea of a very simple weight lifting regimen had terrified me, but in my apartment building's gym with the right equipment, I was able to work out without being surrounded by a lot of fit people at a commercial gym.

By July 2025, I was down 30 pounds.

I had dramatically cut down processed food. In 2025, I had bought a pint of ice cream on only five occasions and not one family-size pizza. I knew that if I brought them into the house, I would not be able to stop myself from eating a pint or a pie in one sitting, no matter how much I told myself otherwise.

I felt in control again. I didn't think of food as my only way to cope. And when I did need to cope, I was learning to do so in healthier ways.

That shift mentally and physically is what made everything possible that summer. Something in me had shifted. I started to gain self-respect and to realize that I deserved to take care of myself. I didn't need to settle. Little did I know that I was coming into a new chapter that would reveal how much I had been growing all along.

It was mid-morning on a typical humid summer day in Georgia. It was Monday, and President Donald Trump was scheduled to make an announcement about crime in Washington. I was sitting inside an office in a public space. I knew that President Donald Trump was going to talk about addressing crime in my old hometown of Washington, but I did not know what was coming.

"We're here for a very serious purpose, very serious purpose. Something's out of control, but we're going to put it in control very quickly like we did on the southern border," Trump said.

I had seen firsthand across dozens of trips to the nation's borders how true that last statement was. The border had gone from three and a half years of 100,000 to 250,000 illegal immigrants arrested per month at the southern border to fewer than 10,000 in the Trump administration's first eight months in office. I knew that Trump intended to crack down on the border crisis when he took office, but even I was stunned at how quick and lasting it was. To me, it meant that his announcement on D.C. crime really stood a chance of succeeding.

"I'm announcing a historic action to rescue our nation's capital from crime, bloodshed, bedlam and squalor, and worse. This is Liberation Day in D.C., and we're going to take our capital back. We're taking it back," Trump said to dozens of reporters crammed into the White House briefing room.

I was sitting in my chair glued to the computer screen, waiting on every next sentence, completely unaware of what was going on around me.

"The process begins right now," Trump continued. "We're getting rid of the people from underpasses and public spaces from all over the city. There are many places that they can go, and we're going to help them as much as you can help. But they'll not be allowed to turn our capital into a wasteland for the world to see."

I mention what Trump said that day for several reasons. As I was watching, tears running down my cheeks and sniffling, I felt seen for the first time by someone who not only cared but was also in a position to do something. Sure, the U.S. Attorney's Office had prosecuted my case. They talked me into a plea deal. My attacker got off so easily. The D.C. Police Department could not even be bothered to make a note in their tally of what happened on April 4, 2020.

Here was someone who not only saw the crime and the victims, but he also didn't like it. And he empathized with the victims and their families. He hated what it had done to us. I never saw that concern from anyone else—not Mayor Muriel

Bowser, not a D.C. city council member, not the U.S. attorney or victim advocate—no one.

That day, I saw the president of the United States through a personal lens, almost as if he had extended a hand to me through the computer screen to say, "I see you. I'm sorry you were hurt. I'm sorry you lost your home, your plans, and your vigor for life. I will make this right in your honor."

I also did not feel guilty for feeling this way. Sure, I was and still am a journalist. I strive to be objective in telling what has happened. But I also vote in elections. And before I'm a reporter, I'm a human being. I'm a daughter, a sister, and a friend. I'm also an American and a former Washingtonian. It's easy to cast reporters into a box and demand they be perfect and rigid in their story-telling and not have opinions. But people are at the center of every story. I was no different.

I wasn't just a reporter who covered crime who herself became a victim. I was Anna, an aunt to now four nephews, the daughter who chats with my parents on the phone every day, the sister who exchanges cat videos of our twin cats that we adopted from the same litter, the friend who sends friends GIFs on Instagram at 3 A.M. when I cannot sleep. I'm also a woman who became a crime victim in the blink of an eye. I'm not a robot. I'm a journalist who first and foremost is a person. I am allowed to feel a certain way about crime in Washington. And I felt seen and heard by the president of the United States that day. And I was grateful.

A few days earlier, I had reached out to the company's opinions editor and asked if he would be willing to run an opinion piece about my experience as a victim of crime in Washington. He said yes. I mentally dragged my feet. Would anyone care what I had been through or what I had to say? I was scared that it could impact my work if I came out with an opinion piece.

But I was more fed up with having to be quiet for five years about the injustices I had seen than concerned about the negative implications of writing an op-ed. So I got down to the real work of telling my story.

I was emotional while writing the op-ed since I was fired up from the press conference earlier in the day. I knew this was the time that I stood a chance of being heard—and also countless other women who have been assaulted and not counted in police stats. My article could also help many other victims who had been hurt and had not reported the crimes, or their attackers had not been found so their cases could not be prosecuted. Other victims who did see adequate justice and still ached from all they had been through could also be heard. Just because justice is done does not mean the victim will know peace. And how much more would it mean not to know justice and still know peace? That was what I wanted to say in the end. This op-ed would be the entry point to sharing my story. Yes, I wanted changes to policing. But at my core, I wanted hurting women to know that the darkest of the darkness does pass. Any crime victim can know no justice and still know peace.

Three days after President Donald Trump's D.C. crime-crackdown announcement, the *Washington Examiner* ran my op-ed. It took off very quickly after I posted it on X (formerly Twitter).

In a string of posts to X, I shared the crux of my op-ed:

> This is the most important story I've told. It's my story. I've waited five years to share it, and I'm ready now.
>
> I'm Anna Giaritelli. The DC police are covering up crime. I know because they covered up what happened to me.
>
> Five years ago, I was violently attacked and sexually assaulted in broad daylight in Washington, D.C., by a homeless man. He served time in federal prison for what he did to me. But if you look for evidence that the attack happened in the @DCPoliceDept crime statistics, you won't find it.
>
> The truth of what happened to me and the D.C. government's role in it is as much a public scandal as it is a personal trauma.
>
> D.C. police covered up the unspeakable wrong that the stranger did to me. Even though a judge sentenced my attacker to hard time in prison, D.C. police leadership would rather deceive the public and appear less dangerous than list mine and countless other sexual assaults on their website.
>
> The extent of crime in D.C. has been debated since Trump announced on Monday that he would take federal action to crack down on D.C. crime.

But if the public wants to have an honest conversation about crime in D.C., the @DCPoliceDept will first have to be honest about how prevalent crime is. Without MPD's honesty about the crimes that it has chosen to hide from its public-facing stats page, the @WhiteHouse cannot get an accurate picture of how bad the problem actually is and adequately fix it.

I was a Washingtonian for seven years. I was saving up money to buy a condo and planned to spend the next few decades in Washington, the intersection of politics and media.

D.C.'s crime problem was something you lived with. You took Ubers and Lyfts, told others if you were walking after dark so they knew when you were home, and knew to be aware of your surroundings, almost to the point of paranoia. (Ladies?)

On a Saturday morning in 2020, I walked out of my apartment on Capitol Hill to mail a package at a post office several blocks from the U.S. Capitol. I put on my sweatshirt and sweatpants then headed out the door.

I never made it to the post office.

Just one block from my apartment building's entrance, I was attacked by a large man well over six feet tall. He charged at me for a reason that I still do not understand. In broad daylight and on well-traveled 2nd Street NE next to Union Station, I fought to get away as he sexually assaulted me. If it had not been for others in the vicinity, including a construction worker named Donny who heard my screaming and ran to my rescue, I don't know if I would be here today.

Why am I writing this op-ed?

Despite my background working with federal law enforcement, it was only through my experience as a victim that I learned personally of two ways that D.C. police and the courts fail the public. I share those now with the hope that they inform the public and leaders to improve how crime is handled and prevented.

My attacker was arrested on the street months later, charged and pleaded guilty to a sex abuse charge nearly two years later.

MPD's "Crime Cards" online statistics page omits mentioning it, though. Do you know what that communicates to a victim? How invalidating that is?

When I asked @DCPoliceDept in 2020 why my incident was not on its crime map, an MPD spokesman said the city includes only first-degree felonies under its crime stats. That would mean that every person robbed, assaulted, or sexually abused in anything less than egregious ways was not included in the total tally. The pain suffered was not severe enough, according to MPD's standards.

In a follow-up email to @DCPoliceDept this week, an MPD spokesperson stated after a back-and-forth exchange that the map includes some sex abuse charges, but not all of them. In my case, my attacker's crime against me, which landed him in prison, is still not listed.

The 54 sex abuses over the past year listed on https://crimecards.dc.gov are a lie. There are COUNTLESS more sex abuse victims who have cases moving forward that the DC police have refused to tally in their counts.

The D.C. Police did do something right. The day of my attack, the police collected my clothes for DNA evidence. About two months later, they contacted me to say they had had a match to the DNA of a homeless man who had been previously arrested.

Police arrested him, but he was immediately released from jail by the judge who presided over the case.

Here I was, a single woman who was attacked a block from my front door. Not jailing him until trial felt like a death sentence. How could I leave my home with him out on the streets, living in a tunnel a few blocks from where I lived?

Trial proceedings were set to begin in the fall of 2020, but amid the George Floyd riots in downtown Washington, it was delayed until early 2021.

Then, the early 2021 start was delayed until the end of that year. The U.S. Attorney's Office assured me it was not because the federal prosecutors were busy bringing hundreds of cases against January 6th offenders.

The man who attacked me was arrested by diligent D.C. police officers on five separate incidents as we waited to go to trial.

> But after every arrest, the judge permitted his immediate release, even when he was caught in public with a machete.
>
> I have thought about these failures by the police and courts for the past five years, but I have not been sure how to bring attention to them. Right now, we have a rare chance to bring meaningful change.
>
> I have shared my story. Will anyone hear it and respond?
>
> Please share my story. Awareness to the problems can bring change.

Among the first to tweet the op-ed was White House press secretary Karoline Leavitt: "Everyone should take 5 minutes to read this incredibly powerful story and example of how D.C. has been failing law-abiding residents and victims of crime. Thank you, @Anna_Giaritelli, for sharing your harrowing experience." Leavitt posted this along with a link to the op-ed.

I was stunned. The top Trump administration spokesperson had shared it, which meant people in the White House and across the federal government would see it, and maybe they would do something. I had to believe they would.

Then another White House official shared the op-ed. White House spokeswoman Abigail Jackson shared it twice along with this comment: "A man went to prison for assaulting me. D.C. Police crime stats show he was never arrested. A must read from @Anna_Giaritelli—thank you for bravely sharing your story."

Things quickly heated up. Columnist Byron York shared the op-ed, followed by members of Congress and the Senate, including Senator Mike Lee (R-UT) and Representative Stephanie Bice (R-OK). Elon Musk shared someone else's post of my op-ed along with Charlie Kirk.

The emails from news media quickly began pouring in. I received five requests from Fox that first day. They trickled in from Newsmax as well as nationally syndicated radio shows and podcasts that all wanted to have me on, including the National Crime Prevention Council's True Crime Prevention Podcast. iHeart radio stations, nonlethal firearm company Byrna Bros, and Washington radio station WMAL also had me on.

The print and digital press was also going crazy for my story. I had emails and text messages from reporters seeking statements beyond what I had said in the op-ed and on X, including those from the *New York Post*, AOL, Newsmax, Fox News Digital, Mediaite, Catholic Vote, *Colorado Springs Gazette*, and the *Denver Gazette.*

Most reporters and TV hosts who had me on did a great job sharing my story and interviewing me. But one reporter, when I said that the attack had ruined my life, pushed back and said that I *seemed* fine.

I was in disbelief that he would push back. He had no idea of the years it had taken me to come back as much as I had and the effort it took to keep my job when all I wanted was to find an easier one out of media. I spoke with him about it the following day, and he said I misheard him. No, I hadn't misheard anything. I heard a man downplaying the horror I lived through and overcame. I was upset, but I was also embarrassed for him.

A different reporter went further than any other to make me feel seen in those interviews. I was doing TV interviews four to five times a day that week and into the next week, as well as hour-long podcast interviews and radio call-ins. I was becoming emotionally drained from rehashing my story and digging into it deeper, thinking of it in new ways that I had not before.

I joined Fox News' *America Reports* with fill-in co-host Aishah Hasnie. It felt like just another interview until she asked the final question. She was empathetic and hated making me relive this story, and it felt genuine.

At the end of our back-and-forth, Hasnie asked, "Anna, are you doing OK now?"

Those six words left such an impression on me. I was taken aback when she asked. I wanted to give a long-winded answer, but knew that was not the time or place.

Later that day, I messaged Hasnie, a reporter whom I had not met while in Washington. I wanted to thank her and let her know how much that question meant to me. I knew that I was a hot-button issue and that the media would jump to run my story. But in the midst of that, this journalist had remembered that I was a person before I was a reporter or a story. It reminded me that how I treat family members and friends of victims who I interviewed for my own stories are people. Ever since my attack, I had treaded lightly when speaking with crime victims or their families. I checked in with them on occasion to say that I was thinking of them or had just prayed for them. I knew what it was like to be forgotten and suffer silently. Now I was reminded of what it meant to be seen by someone else as Hasnie had seen me.

Since I was not living in Washington or a major city, I conducted all press interviews about the op-ed in my apartment. It was nice to be talking about this in the comfort of my home where I was safe, but it also stung a little bit because I would have rather been on set. Not being there reminded me of why I was not in Washington. It seemed ironic.

The peculiar thing about the surge of press that reached out to me after the op-ed ran was in those who did not: CNN, MSNBC, PBS, NPR, the *New York Times*, the *Washington Post*, among many others. Their reporters were actually on X stating that Washington was safe and they had not had issues with crime.

It was a moment when I was disappointed in the media.

The op-ed became the *Washington Examiner*'s most-read piece in months. On X, it collected 3.8 million views and well over 1,200 comments. The late Charlie Kirk had shared a post about it, and so did Elon Musk. Its reach was far and wide.

When I had shared the op-ed on X, I had tagged the D.C. Police Department. I figured this was a problem that they should be aware of, though clearly they already knew.

Many people on X wrote that I was "brave." It was the one word that kept coming back up. I didn't feel brave. I felt embarrassed that it had come to this—writing an opinion piece about the state of crime in D.C. and my experience with the criminal justice system, five years after becoming a victim. But online, people were celebrating my "bravery." I felt that I was straightforward about what I had written and there was nothing brave about it. I was simply sharing my account as a former resident who had experience with covering crime and as a victim.

I shared it with my therapist, genuinely confused about how I was considered brave for writing an op-ed. The idea that I was brave made me think I had done something so big that retribution was inevitable. I was fearful that there would be revenge by those I had accused of injustice.

My therapist asked me to describe how I felt about what I had done without using the word "brave."

"Courageous, brazen, smart, well-timed, challenging, scary, overwhelming."

After listing what I thought, I realized that I actually was describing what bravery is. I remembered that I was not doing this for me; I was doing this for all victims. I believed that God would use my humility and story for His good. I had trusted in Him, and He made me brave.

In the wake of the op-ed, I was approached by and reached out to several editors in the publishing industry. I was referred to several by friends who knew I had not yet begun my search for a publisher, much less an agent who could find one.

As a journalist in the media, book publishing was something I knew nothing about. I had been in the process of writing a query letter on why my book mattered, who the ideal audience was, and how I would work to sell it—everything that agents and publishers would need proof of before signing a deal.

I had started writing my memoir shortly after April 2024, when I announced that I was writing a book on X. I had written about half of the book shortly after moving out of Texas.

Facing my past was challenging, but it became a greater challenge when I decided, in writing about my 2020 assault, that there was more to my story than just that incident. The woman I was that day and as I began writing this book was not someone who had never dealt with serious sexual harassment or assault. (I say "serious" sexual harassment to mean being pushed by a boss to have sex as opposed to being cat-called in public.) I felt as though I would be telling only half of my story if I did not include what happened to me at ages seventeen and in my twenties. But I would run the risk of looking promiscuous. While I believed that no one could blame me for being assaulted in the street in 2020, some people on the Internet suggested that I should dress less provocatively and not go out late at night. They insinuated that I deserved it or walked into the assault. I couldn't win those people over, so I didn't waste my time on them.

But by saying that I made poor choices as a teenager—which resulted in my being assaulted and could have been prosecuted as statutory rape—and discussing the sexual relationship with a boss at work would undoubtedly lead some people to say that these were regrettable decisions and I was trying to play the victim.

Here's what I say to that. I did make decisions at age seventeen that I am responsible for. But what a man did to me that night while I was intoxicated and high remains on him. I didn't lead myself to a car. I didn't open up the trunk and say to get in. I followed him and I lay there, shaking uncontrollably. And I was a minor, too young to have consented. In the eyes of the law, it wouldn't have mattered if I had begged him to have sex. I was a minor, period.

What happened with the supervisor at work could also be portrayed as another gray area. I was well over the age of consent when he came over and I unlocked the door to my apartment. I had received dozens of text messages that caused me to fear that I would lose my job or any chance in the industry if I did not do what he demanded.

I am the seventeen-year-old and twenty-something. That is what makes my story so sad. It would have been bad enough to have never been harassed and assaulted before 2020, but when I walked into the attack on April 4, 2020, I was still struggling to make sense of my past. What happened on that day sent me into a whirlwind of new confusion. I had to unpack all of my past again. I thought I was over so much of it until I was in therapy and realized I had not resolved it or thought it through.

It all goes back to the narrative I told myself the day of the attack: bad things happen to me, I'll never get a fair shake, good is not coming my way, and I'll never be loved because every guy wants one thing and then moves on.

That is the confusion that sexual assault victims live with, particularly those who are assaulted early in life. They learn, without even realizing it, that they're storing this lesson away in their minds, and this is the kind of treatment they can expect.

A victim will need to relearn her value as a woman, a human being, and in relationships, which is a challenge that I and so many others face following assault.

No one just gets over these things that have been learned subconsciously. An assault victim doesn't just fall into a good relationship without first learning how she got into this backward way of thinking as a result of what she has lived through. She would need to take steps to ensure any new relationship has adequate communication, boundaries that are agreed upon and respected, love and appreciation based on who she is and not what she can do for the other person, and so much more.

Here I am at age thirty-six, finally in a place where I actually trust my judgment. I also respect myself in a way that would make dating a good challenge, and instead, I'm writing a book that may scare off many of the legitimately good guys.

Or maybe I am about to prove that despite the car wreck of a beginning, a troubled start, and a tragic encore, trauma can be redeemed. I've experienced enough healing to the point that I can believe in love and know what it is.

1 Corinthians 13 in the Bible talks about what love is: "Love is patient, love is kind. It does not envy, it does not boast, it is not proud. It does not dishonor others, it is not self-seeking, it is not easily angered, it keeps no record of wrongs. Love does not delight in evil but rejoices with the truth. It always protects, always trusts, always hopes, always perseveres. Love never fails."

Every word in those sentences is the antitheses of sexual harassment and assault. Love is how you view and talk to and treat those around you. You do not hurt them, use them, or abandon them.

True lasting love is possible for all who have also believed that they are not worthy, not enough, or too much. But we first must relearn what love actually is to know how we are to be treated and how we should treat others.

I'm a tree for the forest. What happened to me is not unique. It happens every day, whether it's a congressman propositioning an aide or a college student being assaulted while attending a party. There are countless examples. I'm not trying to normalize it—far from it. But I'm saying we have a problem that women have effectively accepted that one in three of us will be assaulted.

The Rape, Abuse & Incest National Network (RAINN), the largest anti-sexual violence organization in the United States and best known for starting and operating the National Sexual Assault Hotline, reports that every 74 seconds, someone in the United States is sexually assaulted. Every nine minutes, a child is that someone. The following statistics are shared on RAINN's website:

> More than two-in-three sexual assault victims are between the ages of twelve and thirty-four.
>
> An estimated 17.7 million American women have been victims of attempted or completed rape as of 1998.

Can you even begin to comprehend how many women in America right now have experienced this?

We have spent decades advocating for men to stop assaulting women and teaching women physical self-defense. If we cannot convince all men to treat women as equals, not objects, and to stop harassing and assaulting them, then we need to create a culture among women that puts them in a far better position to counter the attacks they may face rather than just telling men to cut it out. I'm not talking about more self-defense classes for women. I'm talking about a revolution in what type of culture we are willing to accept for ourselves. We live in the United States of America, and nearly 18 million women have been victims of attempted or completed rape, as of 1998.

I'm done accepting that as normal.

CHAPTER 13

LIVING A COMEBACK STORY

I was working in September several weeks after writing the op-ed when my phone rang from a number I did not recognize. It was a 202 number, meaning that the caller was in or from Washington. I always answer such calls.

It was someone from Senator John Cornyn's office, a Republican from Texas. Cornyn's aide shared that the senator was putting together a press conference to take place at the U.S. Capitol in Washington to talk about crime in the city. She asked if I would be interested in attending and speaking at the conference alongside the senator and other lawmakers who could attend.

It was a no-brainer. "Yes!" I thought in my head. "I will be there!" But I needed to check with my company first. I had entered into an awkward situation after writing the op-ed—I had become the story. It was not a great look for a newsroom or reporter, but I had tried to stay focused on presenting my story, recommending important reforms, and speaking on behalf of victims, not weighing in with an opinion on politics related to crime.

Sexual assault is the most underreported of crimes, and women who speak out as victims are incredibly rare compared to those of other crimes. I had a chance to reach people not just with my call for a change in how D.C. police track crime, but also with a message of hope to countless women across the country who had also survived sexual assault.

The company relented but asked that I note at the press conference that I was not there to endorse a bill or a lawmaker, but only to share my experience. I agreed.

A few days later, I was on a plane headed to Washington Reagan National Airport. I had asked my mother to meet me there, but she could not get off work, so I went alone. So much of my journey has been solo, and this was one of those times when I resented having to do it on my own.

I worked while traveling to Washington and made it into town the evening before the press conference. I checked into my hotel downtown and ordered dinner to be delivered. I then rewrote the remarks that I would share the following day. I was ready for my moment.

As I was lying in bed waiting to fall asleep, I began to feel sick. Within an hour I *was* sick. I spent much of the night in the bathroom, waiting for morning to come. I didn't know what had caused my sudden illness. It didn't seem to be nerves, because I was calm and confident about what I was doing in Washington. Could it have been food poisoning or a stomach virus that I picked up while flying?

In the morning, I told my editor that I would be flying out immediately after the press conference instead of staying through the next day because I was very sick. I wanted to get back home rather than be stranded in a hotel bathroom for another 36 hours.

Flying while sick seemed impossible, but I was focused on getting home to my own bed and bathroom.

But it felt like a test. Of all nights to get sick, here I was before this huge occasion where I would be speaking at the Capitol. It was literally a once-in-a-lifetime opportunity.

I didn't eat that morning or even have any coffee. I was running on very little sleep and would have to stay awake without the help of caffeine.

I dressed in a brand-new suit that I had purchased a few days earlier. I felt terrible and tried to convince myself that I was fine mentally. If I could keep my mind on what I was doing in Washington and not on whether I would suddenly get sick in public, I could stay focused and somewhat relaxed. If I suddenly got sick during the press conference, it would be OK. It wouldn't be life-ending, even though it would seem to be. I took a ride-share to Capitol Hill that morning where I met up with former Congressman Mark Walker and his wife, Kelly.

My connection to Mark is a funny one. About fifteen years before this press conference, I met Pastor Mark Walker in Greensboro, North Carolina. I had just graduated from college, and my parents had moved across the country from Oregon to North Carolina to be closer to family. I had moved with my parents and started working full-time in retail to save up money, hoping to return to Washington to pursue journalism.

My uncle was a senior pastor at a church in Greensboro, and our family had been introduced to the worship pastor, Mark Walker.

Fast forward to 2013 as I returned to Washington. I was an intern at Roll Call. I learned that Walker was one of several candidates in the crowded primary for the congressional seat that included Greensboro. He was up against a number of solid challengers. He was seen as the outsider who did not have a chance. But something told me that Walker would win. I kept my mouth shut because I knew how nutty I would sound to the tenured politics reporters around me.

Sure enough, Walker won the primary and went on to win the seat and head to Congress. Within a couple of years, he was named chairman of the prestigious Republican Study Committee.

Our lives did not overlap much while in Washington, but Walker and I kept in touch occasionally and would sometimes run into each other.

When I was invited to speak at the Capitol in 2025, I shared the news with my aunt and uncle, who knew Walker well. They shared the news with him and told me to reach out to him while I was in Washington. He was in the process of being confirmed by the Senate for a new position in the Trump administration.

On the day that I was set to speak at the Capitol, he was supposed to appear in a Senate confirmation hearing, but it had been canceled at the last minute. When I reached out, he said he and Kelly would be happy to meet up beforehand and keep me company. It felt as though the stars had aligned since my parents couldn't be with me. Someone I knew would be there to support me.

I met Mark and Kelly on the House side of the Capitol grounds. He led us underground into the belly of the Capitol.

We walked to the Capitol dome and I looked up with reverence. It was a special spot that I had walked through countless times before.

On the way through, we stopped by the House Speaker's office for a private moment on the balcony that overlooked the National Mall. Getting out onto the Speaker's balcony was a bucket list item for many Washingtonians, and this was my first time out there.

It also gave me a chance to catch my breath and refocus before I would speak in less than an hour. I looked out at the Washington Monument and the Lincoln Memorial. I was really here, standing at the literal center of Washington, overlooking the city. It was a full-circle moment.

Taking the step of speaking out that day was different from what I had done in the op-ed. It was a new call, specifically to lawmakers here and everywhere, to protect victims and adequately represent them. I was hopeful that speaking out would help bring about change in how the courts dealt with sex offenders. I also hoped it would lead the D.C. police to be transparent about all crimes committed in Washington.

But I had been in Washington and worked in these circles for a decade at that point. Deep down, I was fearful that my hope for these changes would be dashed and that nothing would be accomplished from the press conference.

I had looked at victims of other crimes who spoke at Senate and House press conferences in the past. Lawmakers sought to make examples of them and how they were impacted by policies. But now I was on the victim side. And I felt that I did not have much reason to believe that anything would change. I wanted to err on the side of pessimism rather than optimism, because at least I could then avoid great disappointment.

We stayed outside on the Speaker's balcony for a few minutes and then headed back under the dome and north to the Senate side of the Capitol. I took a final deep breath of the warm air outside and headed in.

I knew from covering many press conferences that included victims of crime or of other issues that I ran the risk of being forgotten afterward. Lawmakers often brought in ordinary Americans who served as examples for the points they wanted to make, and in this case, I was the ordinary American.

What I had not known until now was how much it mattered that I had the chance to share my story on such a large stage. Even if I were forgotten after that day, and even if only a few people heard my story, I had been given a chance to speak as an American to other Americans in our nation's most revered building. No one can ever take that away from me, even after the spotlight shifts away from this issue.

Before the press conference, I spoke privately with Senator Cornyn about what I had been through and what I was hoping to see changed. He expressed his condolences for how the system had failed me. I'd interacted with the senator in person at press conferences several times in Washington and Texas, so I had limited rapport with him, which I figured was better than nothing.

We headed into the press conference room. I stood at the front alongside Senator Cornyn and other senators who trickled in and lined up next to us. The senator introduced me, and I shared my statement. I read from note cards and tried to speak slowly.

Mark and Kelly stood alongside the media. I made eye contact with Mark early in my remarks, and he put his hand over his heart as if to say, "Speak from your heart." It reminded me that this wasn't about convincing people of the need to change policy or that sexual assault should matter more to Americans. It was about sharing my story and letting people decide for themselves.

Senators continued to trickle into the room as the press conference got underway. Each lawmaker took a turn speaking. I felt seen and believed by the senators, especially the women senators. Women see and understand each other in a way that men can't, and that's not a putdown on men. It's just the uniqueness of being a woman. It's also what made the male senators standing behind me so significant; they had no idea what it was like for a woman to be sexually assaulted, and yet they cared enough to be here.

I was called up to the microphone, and I began my remarks:

> I'm a news reporter, so I don't endorse policies or politicians, but I wanted to take this opportunity to speak to the issue of D.C. crime today. I'm here to talk about an important subject. I'm grateful for this invitation.
>
> Like many of you press here today, I moved to D.C. to pursue a career in political journalism, and D.C. quickly became my home. I was here for seven years, and I planned to stay for years to come. I'd been saving up for a condo, and that changed in 2020. I was a few blocks from here, actually, at Union Station outside where we are today at the Capitol walking to the post office to mail a package

on a Saturday morning when a man attacked me in broad daylight on the sidewalk with other people around. This man lunged at me. He grabbed me and pinned my arms down. I was helpless and powerless to fight back against him. He sexually assaulted me in public on the sidewalk. I screamed for help. He screamed over my voice, drowning me out. I truly thank God people were there and got involved and saved me that day.

He got away that day, but DNA on my clothing led D.C. police to him. He was already in the system because he had a criminal record. Three months after the attack, police were able to find him on the street. They informed me that he was homeless and living about two blocks from my apartment building, and they arrested him. It was great news until the following day, when I heard from the U.S. Attorney's Office, he had been released from jail at the judge's discretion. He had returned to living on the street, blocks from my apartment building.

I didn't feel safe, and so I moved away from D.C. to Texas. So to give a shout-out where it's due, in the year and a half that it took for the case to move to trial, police arrested him not once, not twice, not three times, not four times, but five times. And after every incident, the judge released him from jail the following day. One arrest was for exposing himself to a Supreme Court staff member just a block across the street, and another was for wielding a machete in public. The U.S. Attorney's Office prosecuted my case. I was told that, because the jail was crowded, the judge chose to release him so public health standards could be maintained in the jail.

He was finally held in jail when our case moved forward at the end of 2021. In 2022, he pleaded guilty to a sex abuse charge for what he did to me. He went to prison and has since been released. He served about two and a half years. I found out at his sentencing that he had attacked an off-duty female police officer shortly before he assaulted me. That was included along with the other five arrests into that prison sentence.

So what happened to me, and the D.C. government's role in it, is a public scandal as much as a personal trauma. Even though he went to prison, the D.C. police stats show that no crime occurred. I had no idea D.C. police were covering up crime, and continue to do so, until I became a victim. I looked for my own crime stats and found nothing for sex abuse charges except first-degree and certain second-degree charges on the crime map. Why didn't I count, and how many more women and men and children have not been counted? At a time when D.C. crime is being addressed, I ask how can we understand the problem and the breadth of crime when D.C. police are covering up the stats? How can we fix something when we don't know how bad it really is?

What happened to me was humiliating as a woman, and it was disgusting. Yet the way I was treated by the police sent a message that what happened to me didn't matter. I'm here today for the victims who D.C. police refuses to count. I think every victim deserves to be counted, because there are no big victims and little victims—there are just victims. I'm here for the uncounted ones today. Thank you for your time, and thank you, senators.

After my remarks, Senator Cornyn stepped to the microphone and spoke about the importance of addressing crime in Washington. He said that the sentence the perpetrator in my attack had received was inadequate.

Because of everything I went through in the criminal justice system, I didn't think I could complain about the length of the defendant's prison sentence. Even though the sentence was a total of two years for my attack, the subsequent five crimes, and his previous assault of the off-duty female police officer, I wondered who was I to say that two years wasn't enough? So the comment by Senator Cornyn made me feel justified in thinking that the legal system had not done enough.

I spoke with Mark and Kelly again and to a coworker who was on site to cover the event. They said I had done a good job. But what was a good job? Would anything actually change? I was being so hard on myself, putting on unnecessary pressure to speak eloquently and emotionally to stir up actual change in Washington. If change did not happen now, when would it? This seemed to be the only chance.

I walked out of the Senate wing of the Capitol and back out into the sunshine as though nothing extraordinary had happened and that it was just another day.

I headed north toward Union Station, which was where I had been attacked in 2020. The first person I called was my father. I told him jubilantly that I had done it—I had gotten my story out. I shared how hard it had been, given how sick I was the night before.

But I had done what I had come to Washington to do—thankfully, without getting sick while making my remarks. I felt good about it, but now I wasn't sure what to do with myself. I still wasn't hungry. I was afraid to eat, but also felt that I was physically stable enough to stay in Washington rather than immediately go home on the afternoon flight.

I spoke with my father for a bit while standing directly across the street from Union Station.

I told him how funny it was that when I first arrived in Washington in 2010, I flew into Dulles International Airport in Virginia, and my mentor and her husband picked me up and drove me to their home behind Union Station. That was the first building that I remember laying eyes on in Washington.

Here I was now, fifteen years later almost to the very day, looking at Union Station again. It marked my beginning and my end in Washington.

I wondered if the man who had hurt me was still living outside Union Station after being released from federal prison a few years earlier. I doubt that he had seen my message at the Capitol, but if he had, I wondered if he would have recognized me or my story and realized that he was the man I was talking about.

A few weeks later, after returning home, I had a decision to make. I needed to decide how to proceed with the book and how to finish it. The previous month had been grueling in the best way possible. I was still stunned that I had received so much interest and support.

Moving forward with the book was also scary. I didn't know how to explain my goal in telling my story. Was it necessary to have a goal? I wasn't interested in becoming an author, but I was convicted about writing the book because I believed my story was meant to be told. I didn't intend to stomp out sexual assault—I knew that was impossible. As long as people on the planet have free will, they will continue to hurt one another in horrible ways. But I also believed my story could have larger implications if I shared it.

I was not and am not trying to create the next "MeToo" movement. I honestly do not believe that I in my own power could have that large of an impact. But I pray that my life and story submitted to God will be used by Him as He sees fit.

In writing out the rest of my story, I would pour out my heart in a memoir. I would describe the struggles I had already faced with the belief that my story could help girls and women avoid the same heartaches that I had. If one woman reads this book and tells me, "I, too, was faced with a boss who pressured me to have sex with him, but I thought of your story and knew that I had choices," I would consider this to be a success. I wanted to see one woman spared from assault. And I wanted to see one victim decide she could be a survivor, not a victim.

I do hope this book sells big. I have such outrageous goals for it and my story that if I were to tell someone on the street, they might laugh at me.

But as I've written, I've grown more concerned about women and girls. I want to be part of the solution to this assault problem. I want to prevent harm. If a woman reads this book and learns to recognize harassment and is able to avoid potential abuse, she will never know the pain and anguish of what she avoided. She won't know what she has been spared—but survivors will know.

No amount of money I might make from book sales or best-seller lists can top that kind of impact.

Assault takes so much from a victim, but it is often years down the road before she realizes the extent of the impact. She doesn't know how bad the damage is at the time of an assault until she lives through its aftermath, day after day, month after month, year after year. Just when it seems that she's OK and back to normal, she realizes that she's uncovered a new effect of that trauma. It feels like whack-a-mole.

I say that not to scare anyone reading this, but with the hope that my story will help others to pursue healing while not avoiding the pain. It sucks, and it's unfair. Are the men who hurt me now in therapy to deal with their guilt? I doubt it.

My own journey is not over. I hope and believe that the pain I still occasionally face will continue to diminish. Such pain goes completely against the life, hope, and love that I know as a follower of Jesus and as a woman who is loved by many others. And I no longer believe that bad things always happen to me.

I am living a good story. A comeback story. A redemption story. Good things do happen to me. I believe that no matter what is *done* to me, I am responsible for my response. I get to *choose* where my story goes from here.

There is no finish line in my journey, but there was a point when I came to believe that this life now, with all of its ups and downs, is better than it was on April 3, 2020; or before the harassment at work in Washington in the 2010s; or in March 2007, before the party assault.

I am ashamed of what men have done to me, but I do not live with shame. It is their shame to bear, not mine. The pain and shame have been redeemed. I could not have imagined this in the past, but I get to proudly share it now. It is possible.

So where do we go from here?

In late October, I received a call from the White House. It was not the press office, which is the one I normally work with as a reporter. It was the second time the White House had reached out to me after hearing about my story.

On the other end of the phone was a White House staff member who asked how I was doing. I was not sure where to begin or how much he knew since I hadn't spoken to him before.

I told him that it had been three and half years since the defendant in my case was sentenced to federal prison and that he was out and back on the streets. I shared that I was no longer living in D.C., but I was still working for a Washington-based news outlet.

Then he asked what I would like to see happen in light of what I had experienced. His question took me by surprise.

"What *would* I like to see?" I thought.

This is what I have thought about. It's kept me awake at night and sometimes continues to do so. My heart is in making things better for women. The more I think about this loaded question, the more passionate I become.

I felt unworthy answering the question, as if I were supposed to have the right answer or a legislative solution. Don't get me wrong—he had asked the *right* question.

The answer I'll give now is in line with what I told him on the phone.

Five years before this, my therapist had asked what my dreams were. I couldn't come up with any, but after several years of recovery and adjusting to my new life outside Washington, I have begun to dream again.

But I have a bigger dream, one that is not about me.

I dream of a society where sexual assault and harassment are not tolerated. But I know we will never see that on Earth because we are all human beings who get to make our own decisions. Some people decide to help others and some decide to hurt others. We cannot control the decisions of others. We can enforce the law, so when someone does harm to another person, he or she is swiftly and thoroughly prosecuted and the public is protected.

So what is a realistic dream in my case? Are dreams ever realistic?

If people in authority will not care about fairness and justice, they need to be pushed by the public until they can no longer ignore the pressure. If the law is about justice, then shouldn't all parts of it be fair? When it comes to the crime stats in Washington as collected and reported online by the Metropolitan Police Department, those stats should be accurate and complete. Even in looking at the stats right now, the numbers are broken down by incidents, yet it is difficult to determine how an incident is defined. Is an incident a call to 9-1-1, or is it police responding to a situation and filing a report? Is it when someone has been arrested? Is it when police charge someone or when someone is convicted?

My attack checked off all of those boxes, yet it is not listed on the crime stats page. If it's worthy of someone being sent to prison, it should certainly be included in the crime stats.

I hope D.C. Mayor Muriel Bowser, now in her third term, realizes how this compounds the hurt on those who have been physically hurt by criminals. The whole point of law enforcement is to enforce laws and protect people, particularly those who have been harmed by criminals.

Yet the MPD is not protecting victims. D.C. police had a terrific opportunity this summer when the president cracked down on crime in Washington. They could have said, "We haven't been clear with our stats, and as one reporter pointed out, they don't count all victims." They also could've said, "We are going to update our stats page going forward. We will color code the map with a pin for each incident, not a vague color for different regions of the city." They could've broken it down by pins for 9-1-1 calls, police responses, arrests, charges filed, or convictions. That would give the public the clearest picture of crime in the city, as well as how charges are pleaded down, and how many cases actually make it all the way through prosecution.

The mayor could still do that. She has the authority over the D.C. police department to impose any changes she'd like. I hold her personally responsible for this oversight.

I dream of the day that the mayor's office and the D.C. police department announce that they have changed how crime stats are reported. I dream of getting a phone call from the mayor herself saying, "Anna, you are counted in the stats now, as well as X number of previously uncounted victims like you. What happened to you matters, and we're sorry it happened. We're also sorry we didn't count you, and now we've made it right."

I also dream of judges who put victims first. I'm a believer in redemption. There are a plethora of reasons why judges make decisions. While I don't fully understand why they make the decisions they do, I hope they think of victims like myself as their daughter or wife when deciding whether to let a convicted criminal back onto the street. I hope they take time to consider how releasing a violent criminal back on the street, near where the victim lives, will impact that victim. I hope we can find bigger solutions to these problems and that the public will stop electing judges who show no regard for victims.

When I spoke with the White House aide, he asked if I felt like Washington was safer now. I had gone back to D.C. the previous September and was driven around downtown. I told him honestly that it didn't feel different to me as when I left in 2021.

I had not seen any federal police or the National Guard out and about—even outside Union Station. I saw homeless people living on the street in the same places as always. There was a lot of Washington that I didn't see, and I know that federal and local police made thousands of arrests during the summer crackdown. But I told the aide that I wanted to know the Trump administration's longer-term plan for safety in Washington.

What would Washington be like in six months or in five years when Trump was long gone from office? How would the city be safer after the release of thousands of arrested criminals? I appreciate what the president and his administration have done and continue to do about crime in Washington, Chicago, Memphis, and other places. Law enforcement has to be one of the most challenging jobs in America. If anyone is sick of crime, it's got to be police officers. But as much as victims and nonvictims want crime addressed, the police must want it even more. How do they want this to be addressed long-term?

As of writing this, three months have passed since I spoke with the White House staff member, and I have not yet heard about how the president plans to keep crime down going forward. I received an invitation to a holiday open house at the White House in December 2025, which I attended with my parents by my side. Going back to Washington again is an important step for me. I went back and got to see the Christmas decorations inside the White House, but was disappointed there was no one to speak with. The White House sent me a thoughtful but meaningless pity gift for what I'd been through when all I wanted was real change to the criminal justice system in Washington, a place where the president actually has the authority to bring about some of those changes.

I have a bigger dream for women as a whole.

We have lectured men a thousand times on the need for consent, against having sex with an intoxicated woman, of not using a position of power to force a subordinate for sex, and everything in between. Still, we see harassment and assault continue.

I believe as women, we must focus on what we can do for ourselves. We should continue to help men understand how to advocate for and protect the women they know. But it is up to us to protect ourselves. I'm not necessarily talking about taking self-defense classes to prevent attacks. I'm suggesting that we mentally and emotionally prepare ourselves, knowing that we will likely face sexual harassment or even assault in our own lives. Are you on guard, and do you know how to be vigilant and how to respond if you are threatened? You cannot rely on a company's sexual harassment training. That is solely meant to protect the company's interests, not yours.

I didn't know at the time of the encounter with the boss at work that I had legal options that the company had not disclosed to me. I would have had a solid case for harassment in the workplace, but my company's sexual harassment training materials made no mention of that at the time. The company's materials shared only the best practices for actions that would do the least harm to them. I was not aware of the statute of limitations in effect for filing a harassment complaint. In my case, it was one year. My chance at justice was long gone when I found that out. State laws vary, but a quick Google search could be the difference between forcing a company to make it right when a fellow employee has done wrong and having to live with the thought: "If I'd only known I had options."

It's up to women to know these things and to think clearly in a situation. I hate saying that, because it puts the responsibility on us. A woman should be able to walk down the street in any outfit she chooses, but unfortunately, some men on the street will see that outfit as an invitation to harass or even assault her. I've come to realize that I want to put myself in as few risky situations as possible. It means if I sense something unusual or concerning about a man, I will stop and think about it. Our intuition as women is unmatched, and that intuition is not a fleeting feeling—it is telling us based on evidence it has been collecting and piecing together that this is not a good person or situation, as the book *The Gift of Fear* explains. It's up to us to pause and think through it and see the possible harm rather than walk blindly into it.

If the CEO of my company had asked me out to dinner late at night in the nightlife district, I would pause before agreeing. I would consider why he was asking me out one-on-one, late at night, in an area of town where we would not run into coworkers, or where drinking would be encouraged. So often women don't want to be a bother or be difficult, but we have to be for our own good. We are all sick of hearing about sexual assault. It's time we lived like it. We must stop living under assault. I'm over assault. We're all over assault.

My dream is to talk about all of this—to see women empowered, to see healing, to prevent harm, and to enable them to thrive, not just survive.

I have a dream for myself. I want to show women that they can do hard things. The secret to doing the hard thing isn't in what I say—it's in a woman's willingness to empower herself.

The right person to bring these issues to the light is the one who will talk about it honestly, transparently, and wisely. I am but one of many women survivors of sexual assault who are done accepting the status quo. This is not some cheesy movement. It's our *lives. We are sick and tired of being sick and tired.*

I see much good that can come from leaning into this discussion. It can bring healing for girls and women, and understanding for boys and men.

Sexual harassment and assault are out of control in America. That means the shame, despair, and suffering among girls and women are also out of control in America. Millions and millions of women from the Pacific to Atlantic have experienced harassment and assault. Your neighbor, your sister, your professor, your babysitter, your teammate, your daughter, your grocery store clerk, your realtor—it just keeps going.

This is your call to dream. Maybe someone hurt you yesterday or five decades ago. Grieve it good and hard. Grieve all the things you lost as a result. And then as you're ready, start taking steps forward, even if it's in blind faith that you can overcome. It is time to get out of the victim's dugout and step up to the plate.

Start taking steps forward minute by minute, day by day, and year by year—and one day you will realize you're living in an answered prayer. You're living in what was once a dream.

I remember that day for me. I was living in my new home on the East Coast in the spring of 2025. I realized I had not ended up there by chance or because I was not happy in Texas. I began to dream while in Texas. It was Christmas 2023. I was sitting on a couch in a Nashville home when I said to myself, "I dream of living in a beautiful town by the ocean that reminds me of a Hallmark movie town." I dreamed of a life by the sea in a small town with beautiful big trees and Spanish moss waving in the wind. I dreamed of a life that seemed too good to be true. But then I wondered why it couldn't be true.

I was standing in my apartment fifteen months later when I realized that I was standing in my dream. Somehow, by God's grace and providence, the worst experiences of my life were overshadowed by His goodness. He led me to a life that is now so much better than the one I had accepted for myself. It's why I can say that the worst day of my life is now one that I can appreciate.

I've only just begun to dream, and I can't wait to see what comes next.

ACKNOWLEDGMENTS

To God be the glory. While this is my story, I am but an instrument for His good.

Saja

Tara Smith

Mom & Dad

Virginia Hu

Stephanie Kelly

Rebekah Brately

DJ & Brooke Giaritelli

Lizzi & Jeffrey Hammer

Joe and PJ Giaritelli

Marianne Shirilla, Amy Oliver Price, Shelly Morton

Carolyn Bolton Forman

Marisa Schultz

Allison Nielsen

Jamie Higdon

Teddy and Ava

Asbury University

Elizabeth Anchundia Castellano

Tom Freiling & Christen Jeschke

To those whose stories have had a significant positive impact on me:

Chanel Miller—Joanna Gaines—Megyn Kelly

www.ingramcontent.com/pod-product-compliance
Lightning Source LLC
LaVergne TN
LVHW091146080826
845145LV00008B/2272

* 9 7 8 1 9 6 9 8 2 6 3 3 7 *